When the Menu is Manna

When the Menu is Manna

ENCOUNTERS WITH GOD IN EVERYDAY LIVING

Stacia Bell

ISBN-13: 9781519697943
ISBN-10: 1519697945

The Invitation

REGARDLESS OF WHERE YOU ARE in your journey, *When the Menu Is Manna* captures life's common issues and reminds us of God's desire to show up in the midst of them. That's right: our Heavenly Father longs for us to see His hand in every aspect of our lives, so that He may pour out upon us His treasures of truth—gifts that are meant just for us in whatever situation we may find ourselves. No one understands better than God that relationships, parenting, careers, and many more things that affect our daily lives can be very challenging and sometimes seemingly hopeless. Through my personal experiences, shared within the pages of this book, may you find affirmation in the fact that in the midst of it all, our loving Savior desires nothing more than to be present in our everyday lives. It is as simple as that. He just shows up! My prayer is that your heart will be encouraged and your mind challenged to look for and apply His truths in your everyday experiences.

About the Author

STACIA BELL LIVES IN NORTH Texas and has spent the past twenty-two years working in the fields of both elementary and secondary education as a classroom teacher and school administrator. She holds a bachelor of science in elementary education and a master of education in educational leadership. Currently, she serves on the staff of Christ Academy Christian School, working with secondary students. She has been married for twenty-seven years to her husband, Kenneth, and has two adult daughters, a son-in-law, and one grandson. In her spare time, she loves to write and has a passion for sharing the hope people can find in Christ through her personal stories of everyday living.

To my family
Kenneth, Emily, Betsy, Hunter, and Jack. I love each of you with all my heart.

With Gratitude

Jana Maroney, my friend and sister in Christ, I am grateful for your continuous encouragement on this journey.

Table of Contents

Introduction

It must have been some kind of trip. Making the trek across desert lands, heading to an unknown place that had been promised to them with tour guides they hardly knew. Just two and a half months into the journey, resources were *already* running out. Provisions seemed nowhere in sight. They did what any one of us would be tempted to do when a situation seems hopeless: they grumbled. This group, better known as the Israelites, criticized their leaders and even went so far as to blame them for their misery. Without a grateful thought for what they had just escaped, they became filled with discontent. Maybe Egypt wasn't so bad after all, they thought.

Whether the Israelites realized it or not, God was already at work. He had thought of everything, including divinely appointed leaders who would deliver His words telling of His generous provision. Not only this, but also God, being a Father who knows the hearts of His children, knew that they would have many questions about His plan of provision for them.

Maybe their conversation was full of questions and went something like this: "So, Aaron, you're telling us that little birds you call quail will just appear on the ground every evening? And you really think we will wake up to manna every morning? Really? We are simply to gather it? Why can we only gather enough for a day at a time? We would much rather put some aside in case God doesn't come through. By the way, what is manna anyway?"

While they were thinking these very thoughts, or similar ones, God did something miraculous. He simply showed up! The Bible says He appeared in a cloud, rolling across the sky as the news of His provision was revealed (Exodus 16).

Fast-forward thousands of years, and we are really no different. Whether you are a stay-at-home mom, a professional in the workplace, a retiree, or male or female, it makes no difference. We all find ourselves in need of encouragement from time to time. Resources may be limited; doubt may creep in that God isn't big enough to meet the need. But regardless of the situation, we are tempted to handle it ourselves. Like the children of Israel, we long for a sign, an affirmation that God will come through. That He will show up.

When the Menu Is Manna is a collection of writings that bring to life selected scriptures that reveal how God's truth shows up in our everyday lives to meet our needs and help us right where we are. Be encouraged and truly enjoy remembering the times when God has shown His faithfulness to you. Strengthen your own faith by recounting the times He simply showed up! It will amaze you!

> *For great is your love, higher than the heavens;*
> *your faithfulness reaches to the skies.*

—PSALM *108:4*

From Truths to Treasures: Tales of Life

CHAPTER 1

The Popsicle Promise

LIFE IN THE SMALL WEST Texas town where I lived as a child seemed simple. Kids could play outside until fireflies were the only light source. Church bells rang on Sunday, reminding people that it was the Lord's day, and the school cafeteria served "real fried chicken" and chocolate pie. Business deals were made with a handshake, and on those long, hot afternoons, just about anything could be solved with a popsicle.

Dad's job as an oilfield worker had drawn us to this small community of about eight hundred people. My mother worked several days a week at Spencer and Maude's Shurfine Foods while I went to school. I always loved going to the grocery store with my mother to shop or visiting her on the way home from school because she always bought me a popsicle. I also liked Spencer. He was an elderly man—tall, thin, and very spunky. He loved to play tricks on me when I saw him. Often, he forgot the tricks he'd already used and tried them again. I just went along with him so as not to spoil his fun.

One particular day as I was walking home from school, I decided to stop in and ask my mother for a popsicle to eat on the way home. When I entered the store, I remembered she was not there that day. I sure did want one, so I began to quickly think of how I could get it. I didn't have any lunch money left. *Hmm.* Then I spotted a display on the checkout counter. It was a selection of counter checks that the local bank had left for its customers to use for purchases. I had seen my mother use the checks over and over, so I thought to myself, *Why not?* With the decision made, I executed my plan. Confidently, I walked over to the freezer and selected an orange one—my favorite. I walked to the checkout, placed my purchase on the counter, and waited for Spencer to tell me the price.

"That will be twenty-five cents, please," he said.

At this, I reached for a check from the display and proceeded to fill it out for my purchase. How I would love to have a copy of that check today! I have no idea what I wrote on it, but apparently it amused him so much that he didn't even ask questions. I handed my insufficient funds to him, he thanked me for my business, and I left the store—popsicle in hand.

I laugh every time I think about this moment in my childhood. However, there is some truth to be discovered in this comical incident. The Bible says we have all inherited a sinful nature and have an "insufficient-funds payment" stamped on us. It is in no way appealing to know that no matter how much wealth, success, fame, or beauty we attain, we can never achieve enough to be acceptable to God or repay Him for what He has done for us. Some might be tempted to think only the immoral people in our world, those who are blatant and public with their sins, need salvation. The Bible clearly states this is just not true. Sin is a part of everyone's human nature, and sadly, we have nothing to offer to remove it ourselves.

Just like I exchanged that worthless check for my treat, we can exchange our old lives for new ones. I am sure someone in the store that day put a quarter in the cash register to cover my debt. Most likely it was Spencer. That is exactly what Christ did. He paid the sin debt of the entire world by giving His life on the cross and rising again to defeat death and offer every single person eternal life.

I encourage you to recall your own commitment to Christ or to think of someone who could receive the spiritual check with his or her name written after "Pay to the Order of," with "forgiven" written on the "Memo" line and Jesus's signature at the bottom. It was written to each of us personally thousands of years ago and is just waiting to be redeemed.

For the wages of sin is death, but the gift of God is eternal life
in Christ Jesus our Lord.

—*Romans 6:23*

But God demonstrates His own love for us in this:
While we were still sinners, Christ died for us.

—R<small>OMANS</small> *3:23*

That if you confess with your mouth, "Jesus is Lord" and believe in
your heart that God raised him from the dead, you will be saved.

—R<small>OMANS</small> *10:9*

For "Everyone that calls on the name of the Lord will be saved."

—R<small>OMANS</small> *10:13*

CHAPTER 2

Becoming Mary in a Martha World

THE LAUNDRY WAS PILED UP again, and I was thinking about the shirt I needed for Monday morning. It was at the bottom of the pile. This wouldn't have been quite so stressful, but Monday was arriving in just a few hours. With a deep sigh and the washing machine humming some late-night tunes, I rounded the corner into the kitchen. It should have been no surprise; I had not darkened the door to the kitchen for more than a few seconds the entire weekend, so why should I wonder at the avalanche in the kitchen sink. Glasses were piled high, odds and ends were hanging over the edge, and a scent that should never be bottled was permeating the room. Close by, I noticed that the litter box was overdue for a change, and from the corner of my eye, I spotted the mountain of ironing that would require several movie rentals to stay on task to completion. Room by room, I felt my irritation growing. A great family weekend behind me had left me on the brink of despair with the mess that I now wished I had attended to in a timelier manner.

I wish I could say this was my first time to be in such a mental state, but sadly that would not be true. As I looked around, I could tell that no one in the family was bothered by the chaos that seemed to be screaming in my ears. Just when I was about to unload, my husband walked through the living room, drinking from a cereal bowl. Obviously, he had not caught my vibe yet.

"Why are you drinking from a bowl?" I asked him, both frustrated and curious at the same time.

He replied matter-of-factly, "There weren't any cups left."

Under my breath, I muttered. I had no words…only thoughts better kept to myself. Things of this nature never bothered him. Somehow, *my* top priorities never made it to *his* list of important things. *How could this disastrous state not be of utmost importance? I* reasoned. Hadn't I just cleaned up this entire house a few days earlier? Now it looked like a cyclone had hit it, and no one was uprooted by it but me. I was about to lay down the law. Get them shipshape. Change the way we did housekeeping business. But deep inside (I was beginning to calm down), I knew this was futile. In reality, it was a silly reason to be so bent out of shape. I asked myself: *What difference will any of this make a hundred years from now. . .or better yet, what difference will this make a week from now or even a few days? How do I really want to be remembered?*

I could see my epitaph now: *Here lies a truly committed woman. So committed that she spent all her free time making certain that she had a spotless house.* Then the voices would trail off because no one could come up with any lasting benefits from my labor.

When considered this way, it sounded a little ridiculous and somewhat pointless to think that cleaning my house meant it would stay that way. If I wanted to be really honest with myself, I knew all too well that we were lucky if our "together look" lasted even a couple of days! I had to face it. There would never be a time when I could say, "OK, all done!" This I knew to be too true, as somebody always managed to produce a dirty cup just as the dishwasher finished the cycle or needed the bathroom just as cleaner went into the toilet bowl or just had to have a drink of water right after I was done mopping, which added nicely formed muddy footprints. No, I had to face it: if a clean house would never be a lasting accomplishment, then what could be?

In Luke 10, the Bible tells the story of Mary and Martha, two sisters and friends of Jesus who were entertaining guests in their home; Jesus was among the guests. While Martha scurried around making preparations, the Bible says that Mary did not help but rather sat at Jesus's feet and listened to His words. Martha became irritated with her sister for not helping. With so much to do and so many people to serve, Martha felt slighted. She went to Jesus to complain, fully expecting Him to take her side. After all, she was doing an important job. To her surprise, though, Jesus did not rebuke Mary but instead reminded Martha that although both were important, there was more to life than cooking and cleaning. Jesus said Mary had chosen the "better part." This must have been a bitter pill for Martha to swallow. Wasn't she up to her ears in cooking and serving others? Nevertheless, Mary had chosen Kingdom work.

It's hard being a Martha in a world that needs more Marys. In John 15:16, Jesus said "make fruit that lasts." In other words, do the work of the Kingdom. Meet the physical needs of people for the purpose of leaving a positive imprint on their lives. Draw near to people to show kindness, especially when they are not kind. Give your time to listen to someone even when you do not have the time. Be a confidant. Keep your word. Most importantly, skip over the frivolous distractions that keep you from seeing that people—*all* people—are dearly loved by our Heavenly Father. If you take a chance and do some or all of these things or even more, you will be choosing the "better part." That is, you will be doing Kingdom work.

There is risk involved if you are of the Martha mind-set. Your sink may be full. Your ironing may go untouched. You may even have to mop twice or swish the toilet bowl a second time. But really, who will care about these tasks years from now? While necessary, none of these will outlast this lifetime. Therefore, I have made a decision. I am going to do Kingdom work. I want the "better part," even if that means drinking from a cereal bowl every now and then.

> *"Martha, Martha," the Lord answered, "you are worried and upset about many things, but only one thing is needed. Mary has chosen what is better, and it will not be taken away from her."*
>
> —*Luke 10:41–42*

> *You did not choose me, but I chose you to go and bear fruit—fruit that will last.*
>
> —*John 15:16*

My Junky Purse Problems

I HAVE TO ADMIT IT. I suffer from "junky purse syndrome." Ever since I can remember, this condition has plagued me. At twelve, the contents of my purse included strawberry passion roll-on lip gloss by Max Factor, $1.25 movie stubs to the AMC theater near my house, and a few stray candy wrappers. By sixteen, I had added a driver's license, my first checkbook, and a cassette tape or two. As a young mother, diapers, cheerios, and juice cups found their way into the bag's contents, as well as a toy or two, just in case. By this time, my purse was dangerously close to outweighing me!

My purse no longer doubles as a diaper bag, so I no longer have an excuse for its condition of disarray, yet I am still afflicted by the syndrome. I forever have to completely dump the contents to find what I am looking for. I trudge through old receipts, hair clips, phone chargers, fast food coupons, and even sticks of gum that have been broken in half. (I only chew a half stick at a time. It's just one of my quirks.) Each time I do this, I get so irritated that I have to rummage through my bag to find something. Repeatedly I vow that I will clean the mess up—yet I don't.

Some time ago, as motivation for potentially keeping a neater purse, I decided to buy a new bag. It was the holiday season, and I found a very expensive-looking designer bag for pennies on the dollar! Thrilled with my find, I was convinced this was just the motivation needed to keep it organized.

Soon after my purchase, while I was on playground duty, an admirer asked about my new bag. She eyed the outside and commented on the designer label displayed by the trademark emblem attached to the front. She commented on how pricey the bag must've been and how beautiful it was. I squirmed a little. I knew two things about the bag that obviously were not apparent to someone looking on the outside only. First of all, by all appearances, it was a beautiful bag, but secretly I knew it was not authentic but rather an imposter. Secondly, it should come as no surprise—the inside looked like nothing less than a portable junk drawer! Trying to be attentive, I found myself hoping she did not ask to see the inner lining! Shortly afterward, the conversation came to a close and we parted ways. As I thought about our conversation, I decided I didn't care so much if she knew it wasn't authentic. What I had really cared about was the possibility of having to let her see the inside. Now *that* would have mortified me!

Why is it that we are so reluctant to let anyone see the messiness in our lives—our inadequacies, mistakes, and, yes, even our utter failures? Jesus warned the Pharisees about placing too much emphasis on keeping the law to find their acceptance by Him. They were warned about the dangers of fixating on keeping outward appearances rather than reconciling their hearts.

> *"Woe to you teachers of the law and Pharisees, you hypocrites!*
> *You clean the outside of the cup and dish, but inside are full of*
> *greed and self-indulgence. Blind Pharisee! First clean the inside of*
> *the cup and dish, and then the outside will also be clean."*
>
> —MATTHEW 23:25–26

Lord,
Life is often messy. I am guilty sometimes of focusing on the outward things to be acceptable to man rather than asking you to cleanse my inner self. A clean heart is what you require, so I ask you to help me focus not on what is good but on what is best. I want to walk in a restored relationship with you regardless of the messiness I am experiencing.
Forever Yours

CHAPTER 4

Teriyaki Chicken in a Kung Fu Kitchen

ONLY A FEW THINGS RAISE the possibility of marital warfare around our house. Cooking is one of them. This small area of incompatibility should have been recognized early in our marriage when my noncooking spouse enlightened me by introducing me to the gospel of cooking according to Ken. It was here I was presented with the truth about some of my cooking faux pas. To begin with, spaghetti should never be mixed with sauce and served from the same dish. Biscuits should be made without fluffy middles, and cookies should be browned (which in theory sounds reasonable, but in practice the translation for browned was burned).

As individual as his hairbrained ideas seemed at the time, I decided to stake my claim by compromising a smidge rather than raising the white flag in total surrender. After all, he wasn't an experienced cook. Actually, he wasn't even a novice. I took control of these seemingly out-of-control opinions by setting the rules we would abide by when cooking the three previously mentioned items. Henceforth, spaghetti would be served separate from the sauce until it was officially declared to be a leftover. Toast would always be an alternative to biscuits, since losing the fluffy middle was as impossible for the biscuit as it was for my own midsection. Addressing the baking of cookies was plain and direct: bake your own. I took into consideration that being a bachelor for thirty-two years had to come with some "set in your ways" thinking, and I was OK with that. I was also prepared to live by these new cooking compromises. But then the inevitable happened. Someone, and it wasn't me, decided to take up cooking.

As a black belt in one style of martial arts, my husband has always been fascinated by Asian culture, especially the cuisine. So it was no surprise when his first cooking project was none other than fried rice. He mastered the art of this dish to perfection, and it was requested over and over again. *OK,* I thought, *he might lose momentum.* But this sudden chef-like success just fueled his cooking fire, and before I knew it, he was going to make teriyaki chicken for the family dinner—not sometime later but rather that very night! I must admit, I was a little apprehensive. *Isn't this too difficult?* I thought. As the process began late that afternoon, I immediately transferred my apprehension to action. As I rattled off cooking advice as if I were a pro, he remained silent. After a few minutes of my proclaiming myself as his cooking coach, he relented, agreeing to my way of preparing the dish, and we began to cook.

About halfway through the cooking time, I peeked inside the oven, anticipating seeing an exquisite dish (thanks to my help). Surely by now the chicken would be browning, crispy, and glistening with the teriyaki glaze I had so confidently basted it with. Yes, it would be a genuine masterpiece that would belong in the next issue of *Southern Living.* Instead, to my horror, I found the clay baker full of chicken, but it was certainly anything but crispy. The baker was full of water. I hadn't allowed for the escape of the water content from the meat. A wave of panic immediately struck me. Fourteen dollars' worth of organic chicken was about to become a feast for the furry friends who made their home with us. I knew I had to say something. If I didn't, the chicken would definitely be ruined.

Reluctantly, after eating a big slice of bitter, humble pie, I fessed up. I felt quite relieved—that is, until our eyes met across the room. I had seen that same look only a couple of times in our marriage. It seemed to say...*I have no words!* "There's frustration brewing here," I said under my breath. I thought about what to do. I knew what to do, but that was not what I did. Instead, I took the approach that any smart wife would take—I offered more advice! Though I didn't have to run for cover, I quickly realized that we indeed had too many cooks in the kitchen and that I should find something else to occupy my time. I gently affirmed his original plan—he did have one—negated my own, and waited it out. When all was said and done, we had teriyaki chicken. It came by way of boiling, basting, baking, and finally grilling, but still—we had it! The next time he makes this dish, or any dish, I think I will have something important to do, like *be quiet.*

The wise store up knowledge, but the mouth of a fool invites ruin.

—PROVERBS 10:14

CHAPTER 5

Last Word or No Words

Speak clearly if you speak at all; carve every word before you let it fall.

—Oliver Wendell Holmes Sr.

*You don't always have to have the last word to realize
one's true intentions; silence speaks volumes.*

—Unknown

REACHING FOR THE PHONE IN my office that morning, I knew this would be a tough conversation. Before agreeing to the phone conference, I had researched the situation, written down all the facts, looked at policy, and planned how I would deliver what I needed to convey. As had happened on similar occasions in the past, a few seconds into the call all the constructive measures I'd attempted to put in place to make this a productive meeting went awry. For the next several minutes, I found myself hoping that at some point this unhappy person would come up for air. Though I did attempt to interject from time to time, this was a doomed conversation. So I settled in on my end of the line and waited in silence until this very unhappy soul exhausted his thoughts on the matter. Suddenly, there was silence on the other end of the line followed by a disconnecting click.

To be perfectly honest, I struggled with this ending. Wasn't I entitled to be heard as well? The whole experience was quite unsettling. I would venture to say my opponent felt some self-satisfaction for controlling the conversation. It would have been easy to let myself feel defeated that day, but I held fast to the fact that the outcome would remain and my decision was constant.

Though I had the authority to act regardless of whether he was willing to listen to me or not, I would have preferred conversation first. Since this was not to be, decision time had come. I pondered the idea that having the last word sometimes requires words and at other times it requires silence.

From the day his earthly ministry began, Jesus had conflict. Like the unpopular news I attempted to deliver over the phone that day, Jesus too had frequent contact with difficult people who rejected His message. He could have called in legions of angels to take the hurling insults that weighed on Him emotionally, along with the physical pain inflicted on Him. However, He did not choose to strong-arm His offenders but instead held fast to His purpose and kept His eyes on the will of God, the Heavenly Father. As the world lashed out at Him through mocking, betraying, arresting, and ultimately crucifying Him on the cross, He never compromised the message He had been sent to give or the method by which it was to be delivered. He knew full well His time had not yet come, but soon He would have the last word, and it would become the lasting word that would change humankind's destination if they would believe and follow.

When the right time came, "With a loud cry, Jesus breathed his last. The curtain of the temple was torn in two from top to bottom. And when the centurion, who stood there in front of Jesus, saw how he died, he said, 'Surely this man was the Son of God'" (Mark 15:37–39).

When he had received the drink, Jesus said, "It is finished."
With that he bowed his head and gave up his spirit.

—*John 19:30*

...a time to be silent and a time to speak.

—*Ecclesiastes 3:7*

Remind me, dear God, that I not only do not need the last words in conflict, but sometimes I need no words. Please order my words for the situations I face. Help me to remember it is not a sign of defeat to choose silence or let my words be few.

CHAPTER 6

Why God Has a Supercharged Flashlight

Nothing good happens after midnight.

—DAD

ONE OF MY MANY BAD habits is meandering around the house in dark rooms when I should just turn the light on. This probably comes from years of having a job that requires me to be up and out of the house before anyone else even has to rise. I've experienced the usual stubbing of the toe on furniture that I am sure moved on its own. I've dealt with the plight of deciding whether or not a sock is black or navy, and I once even bore the embarrassment of wearing of two totally different shoes (including height of the heel) outside the house. I have had ample reminders of how dangerous the darkness can be, whether someone has accidentally turned off the light at the base of the stairs before I reached the top or switched off the light while I was in the shower. In both instances, I lost all sense of direction, and the darkness overtook me. You would think I would learn my lesson, yet I continued to enter dark rooms until several nights ago.

I only went into the bedroom to quickly grab my purse. *It is always in the same place, so why waste the time turning on the light?* I reasoned. All of a sudden, about three steps inside, I put my right foot down, expecting the cold hardwood floor to be my landing. I was surprised to feel my foot slide into a gushy ooze of something. Immediately I thought, *I can't move. This is absolutely disgusting. What is it, and where else might it be lurking?* I yelled for help, bellowing about the mess I was standing in. My husband came running to see what all the commotion was about. The first thing he did was switch on the light. In just a few seconds I had gone from not knowing to knowing exactly what I was standing in. Face-to-face with this sickening mystery substance, I quickly figured out who the culprit was: Rosie, our cat. Apparently, she had not enjoyed her dinner that evening and had decided to fully refund us. What the darkness had concealed, the light had made plain for us to see, and it was sickening!

Though my husband was primarily addressing our girls' curfews—and more specifically, the importance of morality and sound judgment—when he said, "Nothing good happens after midnight," I can think of many applications. In Ephesians 5, Paul mentions living in darkness. What exactly is dark living? It may be defined as different things for different people. All in all, it's anything we willingly allow into our lives that contradicts God's word. Are you thinking of something that hits home with you? I sure am!

Sometimes I have to spiritually stumble around in the dark, step into a few messes, and be forced to yell for help because I am walking on the dark side. It's at these times that I justify my actions with human logic and fool myself into believing that if I conceal it, then all is well. Right? No, wrong! God's word promises that His children don't get away with such foolishness! It is at these times that God sends the Holy Spirit to shine like a supercharged flashlight right into the very heart of my deeds or actions, my thoughts and beliefs. God says no hiding allowed! As His child, He just can't leave me wandering around in darkness, because it is spiritually and possibly physically dangerous. Instead, with my willingness and my yielding to Him, He restores me. He calls me a Child of the Light.

> *For you were once in darkness, but now you are light in the Lord…*
> *Live as children of the light and find out what pleases the Lord.*
>
> —*Ephesians 5:8—10*

CHAPTER 7

Working on the House

MY HUSBAND, KENNETH, HAS A wonderful quality. He is an eternal optimist. Unfortunately, I am not. A few months into our marriage, we discussed moving from our tiny apartment to a larger home. I was excited to think of the possibilities. I so wanted an older home with both charm and beauty. I had dreams of a big wraparound porch with a swing, a beautiful staircase, and wood craftsmanship throughout. To me, this would be the perfect place. My husband, on the other hand, kept it simple. He was looking for two features in the perfect home: functional and economical. I thought that meshing our ideas of the perfect place might be a bit difficult. However, I was willing to try.

At this time, Kenneth was looking for a new piece of property to expand his business. He spotted a place right across the street from his current location. It was a four-thousand-square-foot warehouse, and he believed this could be the perfect place for us. I must admit, I had my doubts. It was nothing like what I had envisioned. After visiting the house to check out the possibility, my former words during our dating months—*I would live with you in a tent*—came back to haunt me. Oh, why did I say that? I could have kicked myself! An elderly couple had lived there for over forty years, raising their only son and running a second-hand furniture store from the bottom level, which now held ancient remnants from their working days. I was anxious to see the top floor, since this was where we would be living. There was a staircase, but it certainly was not beautiful. As for the craftsmanship, it consisted of mismatched wallpaper, dingy paint, and dark paneling. The grand, picturesque moment was seeing the water cooler that was mounted in the back wall of the living room.

They were eager to tell us details of each and every room. I found that a little odd. At this point, I was becoming panic-stricken. The mess to me was overwhelming. Kenneth, on the other hand, was quiet and assured that this was *it*. He saw the potential for the warehouse. I saw the cracking plaster, and did I mention there was *no* wraparound porch? Deep in my heart, I knew it made the most sense. It was functional and economical.

We purchased the warehouse soon after our visit. Immediately, we went to work on our "castle of its kind." Days were spent sanding, painting, cleaning, hanging blinds and wallpaper (matching this time), and moving in new furnishings. I couldn't believe it, but it was coming together nicely! Yet this was still not what I expected or thought I should have. I was ashamed of my attitude. We developed a five-year plan for living there. Then I would get my dream house—or some version of it—so I settled in, continued to work on the house, and started the countdown until moving day.

More than twenty-five years have passed, and I stopped counting a long time ago. Our five-year plan turned into ten, then fifteen, and so on. Life happened, and we settled in. Through the years, I have continued to work on the house, changing it little by little and feeling great satisfaction with each project completed. What I failed to realize was that as I was changing the house, it was changing me. We have built our life here, whether we intended to or not. The rooms are filled with our memories, both good and bad.

Like the elderly couple who showed us the house that day, I too can tell you important things about each room, such as where our girls took their first steps and the place I found the much-loved stuffed bear that had been missing for months. I can show you the room that held a beautiful playhouse the girls built with their dad, which eventually morphed into a clubhouse when they were too old for dolls. There's a spot in the kitchen where pictures were taken every year on the first day of school, and Kenneth's front showroom doubled as a roller rink at night since we didn't have a yard.

There are also sounds only we can hear. Sounds of giggling teenage girls during slumber parties and awkward silences when dates arrived for the first time. There is the sound of happy laughter at the announcement of an upcoming marriage and, more recently, the sound of sweet baby cries. The memories are endless, and the creativeness that has been used here has transferred this unsuspected place into a home.

As we are getting older, every now and then we do consider moving. I suppose someday, when we retire, we will sell the house. Maybe I will get that wraparound porch with a swing; maybe the new house will be filled with the finest wood craftsmanship and be a thing of beauty and charm. Maybe not. Funny how it is not so important anymore. Of one thing I am certain. When we hand over the keys and walk away, the new owners will see what I saw that day so long ago—an empty shell—and so it should be. At that time, they will also see the flaws of the house, for it will be stripped of our possessions, our presence, and our memories. We will take all of those with us. The house will be waiting for them to fill it, to perfect it, and to inhabit it, just as we did for so many years.

For every house is built by someone, but God is the builder of everything.

—HEBREWS 3:4

CHAPTER 8

The Itsy Bitsy Spider's Take on Real Faith

I AM CONVINCED THAT THE spider is one of God's creatures we can all take a lesson from. It was bath time, and my ten-month-old grandson was having quite a time in the tub. As he played with cups and colorful balls, I began singing "The Itsy Bitsy Spider." I could tell he was quite familiar with it; he began to put his fingers together to "climb up the spout" and then squealed with sheer delight when we reached the part where the rain "washed the spider out." We sang it over and over, and each time he showed the same excitement as he anticipated again and again the spider getting washed out!

Later, I thought about our bath-time fun and especially about that poor old spider. It seems she could never catch a break. Just about the time she started up the spout, hoping to find that perfect place along the eaves of the house or on a window frame to spin a magnificent web, the rain came and washed her right back down the spout, only to have to start all over again.

Though I had sung this song millions of times with my own children, this time it struck me differently. Maybe I can give credit to senior wisdom, but whatever the reason, that spider in my opinion belongs right alongside the Energizer Bunny. She had enough faith to keep her focus on the possibilities awaiting her once she made it out of that dark, old rusty spout, so she persevered.

Do you sometimes feel washed out by life? I do. It's during the times when the sky is raining down strains on relationships, financial pressures, illness, and other interruptions to our well-being that we demonstrate real faith—or the lack thereof.

James, the brother of Jesus, wrote the book of James to deliver the message of where real faith comes from: perseverance. Real faith is the result of standing through the tests and pressures of life. Though it is different for each of us, our circumstances force our true beliefs out in the open so that all can see what we are truly made of.

In short, evidence of real faith is seen well when we are sliding down the spout!

> *Consider it a sheer gift, friends, when tests and challenges come at you from all sides. You know that under pressure, your faith life is forced into the open and shows its true colors. So don't try to get out of anything prematurely. Let it do its work so you become mature and well developed, not deficient in any way.*

> —JAMES 1:2—4 MSG

CHAPTER 9

By Appointment Only

THERE IT WAS, POSTED ON a sign I pass every weekday on the way home from work:

Reconciliation
3:00 p.m.–4:30 p.m.
or by Appointment

I must admit, just reading this message stirred my spirit a little, but I did not have the urge to stop and go right in to schedule an appointment. After all, I can't even get yearly appointments such as medical, dental, and vision scheduled in a timely manner. However, it did get me to thinking! Scheduling my reconciliation with God? I was familiar with quiet times before God and scheduled Bible studies, but not scheduled reconciliation. If this is to be, what will I do if I fall short between scheduled appointments? With my frequent shortcomings in thought, word, and deed, more appointments than I could keep would be necessary.

Thankfully, someone had already shared with me that no additional appointments would be necessary. God already knew when I messed up. I couldn't beat him to the punch. Unless it was for the sake of repentance and repentance alone, I didn't even have to give him the "hows and whys" of what I had said or done. He already knew. My past, current, and future mistakes were already exposed, and rather than charge them to me, he did just the opposite. He forgave me, and He did this before I even knew I needed it!

This truth is not only for me. God scheduled the ultimate reconciliation appointment on behalf of a world that desperately needed His forgiveness! We had nothing to do with this appointment, and Jesus had everything to do with it. With our willingness to accept the finished work of Christ on the cross, we are reconciled to God. We move from a place of a people who *know about* God to a people who *know* God. No longer separated from Him by our sin, we have the privilege of direct access to the God of the Universe. We have but one intercessor, Jesus Christ Himself, and we can come boldly before the throne of God to find forgiveness, renewal, and restoration in our relationship with Him.

While I still pass this sign every day on the way home from work, I smile and breathe a sigh of relief because...*no appointment is needed!*

> *Therefore, if anyone is in Christ, the new creation has come: The old has gone, the new is here! All this is from God, who reconciled us to himself through Christ and gave us the ministry of reconciliation.*
>
> —2 CORINTHIANS 5:17–18

CHAPTER 10

The Sweater Club

I KNEW WHEN WE REACHED the mall that Saturday that I was not going to be able to avoid it. She had been talking about the sweater all week. It was inevitable; we were going to wind up in *the store*. I mentally went through my list of strategies that might lead to avoidance. *Maybe I just won't bring it up*, I thought to myself. *Maybe she won't ask*. Who was I kidding? Right as we stepped into the mall, the dreaded happened. She asked. I tried to put her off by saying, "You have plenty of sweaters, and that place is too expensive." I even used the excuse that never works (I was getting desperate): "You will never wear it." Nothing seemed to appease, so I reluctantly agreed to just take a look at it, knowing full well and taking responsibility for where this was going. "Must be some sweater," I mumbled.

Down the mall corridor we moved, with her walking as if she was going to claim a great fortune and me trailing behind her as if I was going to the guillotine. Once we reached the store, she didn't even look behind her to see if I was still following. Instead, she pulled her size off the rack and began trying it on and admiring it in the dressing-room mirror. It wasn't that I intended to be a total Scrooge while shopping that day, but somehow the look of this item did not meet with my standards of practicality, versatility, and long-term usefulness. All the while, she chattered about how so-and-so had this exact sweater and how she would wear it every day. By now I knew I was being pulled over the commonsense line in this shopping experience. Feeling a little weakened in my stance to resist the purchase, I found that I couldn't ignore the enthusiasm in her voice. I caught the hopefulness in her eyes. I just could not see why this particular garment was so appealing; it didn't appear that spectacular to me. I could tell she believed she would be at the least shunned or worse might die without it. Gawking at the price tag, I went against my better judgment and reluctantly crept in a dirge-like manner into the long line to purchase the sweater, while listening to my preteen's promise to wear it every day.

The following week, she wore the sweater to school. I looked forward to a full report of her acceptance and induction into the "Sweater Club," but not a word was mentioned that afternoon. Caught in a war between my head and my heart—knowing each had a mind of its own that might soon venture right out of my mouth—I willfully decided to keep silent about the issue. I looked for justification for this seemingly foolish purchase, but I eventually came to the conclusion that just getting to wear it and be seen in it *was* the purpose.

Her silence confirmed my conclusion that it was not really about the sweater at all but more about the importance of belonging at her awkward age. There was really no reason to bring it up. I knew in time she would see the shallowness of this type of conforming, but at this stage in her life it meant everything to her. So as long as it wasn't immoral, illegal, or required collateral for purchase, we would take one fad at a time into consideration.

After that week, the sweater hung in the closet far beyond its fashionable state. It was never mentioned again. There were other fads—fuzzy platform shoes, specific backpacks, and probably some other things that have long left my mind years ago. All are symbolic of stepping-stones on the road to understanding that acceptance according to God's standards is much more important than those of the world. I would have to wait for that day with patience, understanding, and guidance. For the time being, though, I did acquire some interesting conversation pieces for yard sales. Sweater anyone?

> *Even as he chose us in him before the foundation of the world, that we should*
> *be holy and blameless before him. In love he predestined us for adoption*
> *as sons through Jesus Christ, according to the purpose of his will, to the*
> *praise of his glorious grace, with which he has blessed us in the Beloved.*

—EPHESIANS 1:4–6 ESV

CHAPTER 11

The Heart of It

SPRING IS TRULY MY FAVORITE season of the year. Time to put away all the dark, drab colors of winter clothing and pull out bright and cheery apparel that seems to announce the arrival of spring. It is a time when somehow a newfound energy starts to emerge. Time to hit the track, wash the windows, plant flowers, clean out closets, and maybe even paint the house! Regardless of the activities chosen, it's about renewal. Sprucing up the home both inside and outside, though important, is symbolic of the regeneration of the heart.

Spiritual deep cleaning begins in no other place than the heart. Jesus shared a parable in Matthew 13:3–9 that illustrated that the heart's condition is directly linked to receiving and accepting God's word. New believers, those who have been in the faith for a long time, and seekers all share the need to hear from God. Maybe for different reasons, but all need to hear from Him. The condition of the heart is the starting place.

Long ago, there was a farmer; Jesus called him a sower. This man had the responsibility of scattering the seed over a field and yielding a crop. That was pretty much all he had to do, and while it might seem like a simple task, sometimes it was quite complicated. Despite the sower's good intentions, as he scattered the seeds, they landed in various places. Some hit very hard ground and became a quick meal for the birds that swooped down to eat them. Some landed on stony ground, and the seeds could not take root. In due time, the hot Middle Eastern sun beat down on the tiny plants, and they simply withered away! As he moved through the field scattering some of the remaining seed, it fell among the thorns and the thistles. For a short time, the plants did take root and began to shoot up, but very quickly the thorns and thistles choked the life right out of the new plants. Finally, some of his seeds did fall upon good soil that had been turned, fertilized, and cultivated in preparation for the arrival of seeds. It was on this particular area of ground that the crop began to spring up. The sower received a harvest that was larger than the total number of seeds he planted.

Deep cleaning the heart is much like the sowing of seed in the proper soil. Like the hard ground, stones, thorns, and thistles, the heart has its own set of deterrents that thwart the message God intends to be heard. Sometimes the heart may be devoted to bitterness and anger that results from being grossly disappointed or having had an injustice committed against it. It is here that the heart is made deaf. It can't hear from God even if it wanted to.

Another heart might have the markings of "Godly talk" written all over it. Perfect words are uttered, and the appropriate spiritual behavior is displayed. This heart can both speak and act spiritually on demand, but really that is all it is—mindless chatter and rote actions. Here the heart is not convicted and is noncommittal.

Possibly there are hearts that battle wandering. Back and forth, they sway in and out through a swinging door as the world lures and promises are chased after. The return is inevitable; the world does not deliver. This is a divided heart.

Even still, like the seed that fell on the prepared soil, there is an opportunity for a prepared heart. When barriers are recognized, removed, stripped away, and buried, a prepared heart can be found. This heart holds nothing back. It is open, attentive, repentant, and still before the Lord. This is a devoted heart.

Create in me a pure heart, O God, and renew a steadfast spirit within me.

—Psalm 51:10

CHAPTER 12

Doing Battle with a Heart of Self-Reliance

When you determine to get your own way, you
blot me out of your consciousness.

—SARAH YOUNG, JESUS CALLING

SHE WAS ONLY TWO AT the time, but if I heard her say it once, I heard her say it a thousand times: "I do myself!" It didn't matter what the task was—eating, dressing, brushing teeth, reading (she couldn't read), and basically anything she set her mind to do—she insisted on doing it herself. Sometimes I would have to bite my tongue and sit on my hands to keep from intervening prematurely. When she had exhausted her efforts, only then did I step in to help. At this point, sometimes it was a real mess to clean up. *Where did she get such a mind-set?* I asked myself. At the risk of being cliché, to answer this question I had to admit that the apple certainly did not fall far from the tree in the area of self-reliance.

For me, resisting the temptation to figure out solutions for every obstacle is hard. Over and over again, the "Thanks but no thanks—I've got this!" mentality surfaces. Thinking and in turn acting with this attitude has never served me well but rather has caused a disconnect in my spiritual navigation system. I've begun to notice that when I am in charge, God is strangely silent. Quite possibly, sometimes He is at the point of biting *His* tongue and sitting on *His* hands while I too say, "I do myself!" Yet He is more patient than I. He waits while I demand my own way, communicate on my terms, and refuse to surrender my will. He stays the course until I come to the end of my schemes and relentless efforts to fix everything. He remains until I come to the end of myself. When I have no ideas or options left, when there are no resources to spare and when no strength is available to continue, that is when God does His most magnificent work in my life. He replaces the cravings for results with the peace of resolve. His resolve. He sends the same message to me—*I've got this*—allowing me to rest in His will rather than my way.

While God did equip you and me to be problem solvers, to seek solutions and to find the joy that comes with personal success, practicing His presence should always be first. When we are in that special place, we are reminded that even though life is happening all around us, we do not have to panic. There is no need for survival mode, either. God, our Father, is asking us to listen for His voice and to wait for His direction. He will always, always say, "I've got this."

Look to the LORD and his strength;
seek his face always.

—*1 Chronicles 16:11*

CHAPTER 13

Halting a Haughty Heart

THAT MORNING, I GREETED HER with a welcoming smile and tried to make small talk as she made her way to the counter. Quickly I realized she was not interested in chitchat. In fact, it appeared she was slightly annoyed by my cheerfulness. Both her facial expression and definite body language sent a strong signal that I should drop my role as the welcome wagon and direct my efforts toward getting to the point of her presence there that day.

"How can I help you today?" I asked, fully expecting a response that would clue me in to what my next move should be. I was taken aback when she responded with two rather direct questions that were spoken aloofly. "Who are you?" she asked. And before I could respond, she spoke again. "Don't you know who I am?" The tone with which she spoke made the hair rise on the back of my neck, and I worked very hard to keep my eyebrows on an even plane and my mouth from twitching. In fact, for a few seconds I had a pretty straight mental conversation with myself: *Who does she think she is talking to me like that? How dare she charge in here like this?*

It was an "angel on the right shoulder and devil on the left" kind of moment. I was fairly certain the latter was winning at this point, because I wanted nothing more than to give her a piece of my mind. I would've loved to explain explicitly that her demeanor was nothing short of being totally offensive and inappropriate. With all the thoughts swirling around in my head, I'm not sure what my face looked like, but I certainly know what it felt like. Then a thought occurred to me: *Didn't she know who I was?*

Quickly, I went into conflict management, but in silent mode. *I'm the adult here,* I repeated to myself. *I'm the professional.* Now I just had to figure out how to act like both rather swiftly. I wish I could say I had a spiritual moment where God showed me exactly what to say. Where He affirmed her seemingly unacceptable behavior, and I was consoled and could now extend mercy. That's not what happened. In my flesh, I shot a glance across the room at my coworker and tried to collect my negative thoughts, check my attitude, and formulate some sort of response that would come across in a manner that would be the exact opposite of the one I was mulling over in my head. When I managed to get my verbal bearings before opening my mouth, I took a deep breath and replied hospitably to both of the rapid-fire questions I had been hit with just seconds before.

"Oh, certainly," I replied. "I should have introduced myself." I did so, and then I continued, "I'm sorry, but I do not think I've had the pleasure of meeting you."

Knowing who I was seemed to satisfy her, and after she informed me about who *she* was and the purpose for her visit, I did the only logical thing I knew to do. I gave her clearance and allowed her into the interior of the building. With my blood still boiling, not so much at what she had said but rather how she had said it, I wanted nothing more than to justify my ill feelings. I certainly had not seen this coming, and I thought I was very undeserving of such treatment. So I recounted once more: *Is she considering my position? Is she even thinking about the possibility that I too have some importance attached to my name?*

After several more experiences that year with this person, though her behavior never changed, I began to understand more of what this situation was meant to accomplish. The true takeaway was that I had haughtiness hiding in my own heart. I'm sure it was no surprise to God that it would take more than one occurrence for me to get the message, but each time I found myself in this situation, I sensed the Spirit of God present. He began to calm my mind, which left to its own device would have declared war. He carefully measured the words I needed to say in the moment, and He provided me with genuine understanding and peace that I could emulate. It was a difficult but valuable lesson. I clearly had my own version of self-importance revealed by my attitudes that surfaced. It was time for transformational thinking…not once but on a daily basis.

Isn't it wonderful to know that we are all equally significant to God? As His children, born into a personal relationship with Him, He knows our name, so it is extremely insignificant if others do or do not. God cares not what position, educational level, success, or lack thereof belongs to us. To Him, we are esteemed as sons and daughters of God with full rights to belong to Him eternally. In short, He thinks we are pretty great! We are fully accepted.

Allowing a haughty spirit to invade our hearts provides a foothold for self-centeredness. It doesn't happen overnight but rather over time. Little by little, we move ourselves onto the throne of our lives, which leads to lawless thinking and ultimately self and/or spiritual destruction. Both are unable to hear the gentle beckoning of the Spirit of God to pause, listen, learn, redirect, and walk as a servant of Christ rather than in service to ourselves. Our response when dealing with haughtiness dictates who is truly on the throne of our lives.

Not so with you. Instead, whoever wants to be great among you must be your servant, and whoever wants to be first must be your slave—just as the Son of Man did not come to be served, but to serve, and to give his life as a ransom for many.

—*Matthew 20:26*

There are six things the Lord hates, seven that are detestable to him: haughty eyes.

—*Proverbs 6:16*

CHAPTER 14

The Stinky-Speech Syndrome

IT WAS LATE IN THE afternoon when I returned home from a short shopping trip. I did the usual and threw my bags on the table, intending to come back later to unpack them. A few hours later, while in the kitchen I heard the sound of rustling plastic behind me. It was my cat, Rosie. She had jumped into one of the shopping bags. I watched as she took great delight in first picking through the contents of the bag and then deciding she would just sit on them. Contentedly enclosed in the bag except for her eyes that peered out at me, she just sat there for a few minutes motionless. She soon grew bored with this position, at which point she began to try to get out of the bag. I think it was a feat harder than she had anticipated. First, her head popped completely out of the bag, followed by front paws that somehow got tangled up in the bag's handles. I watched for a bit to see if she would be able to free herself. Soon it was apparent that I would need to free my fur baby. Was she ever glad to be out of that bag! So I guess you could say I literally *let the cat out of the bag*!

God too has something to say about "letting the cat out of the bag." While none, including myself, like to admit that we have been a part of this at one time or another, if we are truthful we would have to agree that we indeed have done just that. At some point, we have shared information that was not intended for us to know and definitely was not ours to tell. The Bible calls this gossip. As it travels through circles of listening ears, it leaves trails of speculation, altered perceptions, and damage to reputations. The subject of this idle talk is powerless to defend himself or herself, and new altered opinions are often formed. However, it is not only the subject of gossip who is hurt; the one choosing to share this needless chatter suffers ill effects as well. The spreading of such talk yields gratification only for a second, yet the effects of this action are long-lasting. Personal integrity, character, and trustworthiness become marred and often affect the ability to have meaningful relationships with others. The book of Proverbs gets to the heart of "Stinky Speech"

Information that someone trusts you with in confidence is not yours to share with others.

> *A gossip betrays a confidence,*
> *but a trustworthy person keeps a secret. (Proverbs 11:13)*

Passing along hearsay and speculations and adding a personal slant about someone or something, whether it is true or not, often leaves a negative or even damaging impression of a person or situation in the minds of others.

> *The words of a gossip are like choice morsels; they go down to the inmost parts.*
> *(Proverbs 18:8)*

Not being trustworthy with a confidence can cost you a friendship.

> *A perverse man stirs up dissension, and a gossip separates close friends. (Proverbs*
> *16:28)*

Breaking someone's trust will cause others to avoid sharing with you.

> *A gossip betrays a confidence, so avoid a man who talks too much. (Proverbs*
> *20:19)*

> *Listen carefully how people speak about others to you.*
> *That's the way they speak about you to others.*

> —U*NKNOWN*

CHAPTER 15

What to Wear: Fashion That Lasts Forever

What you wear is how you present yourself to the world, especially today when human contacts go so fast. Fashion is instant language.

—MIUCCIA PRADA

I MIGHT AS WELL COME clean and admit I am a repeat offender of many fashion faux pas. It all started one day in gym class in the seventh grade, when I was in such a hurry to redress and get to math class that I wore my shirt inside out to class. I could have convinced myself that this was a single fashion error until I looked down at my feet on two separate Sunday mornings only to discover that on one occasion I had worn one navy loafer from two different pairs of shoes, one of which was covered in white specks of paint from a home improvement project. As for the second mishap, it involved wearing not only two different sandals but also two different heel heights. How I managed that still puzzles me.

In earlier years, while raising my daughters, I avoided shopping for myself with them. These trips were less than productive in that I either got home with items I had been talked into buying or I had to admit when they said, "Mom, are you really going to wear that?" and I still insisted, that I should have listened. Now that they are grown, I miss those shopping trips and relish the time when by some chance shopping together still happens. I have come to accept that I need help in the fashion world, and now I am willing to seek it. I march on, knowing that lack of style, mistakes, and stains will continue to plague me. I have learned to accept that even if my outfit is great, I will most likely end the day with a minimum of one stain, be it food, ink, copier toner, or chocolate pudding handprints from one of my little huggers in the cafeteria. Yes, even on a good day I still need help!

If fashion is indeed "instant language," I could be in instant trouble if I am judged by the way I look sometimes! The upside to my dilemma is that God gives fashion advice that is constant, timeless, and in no way dependent on my own fashion mishaps. No trends or latest styles to contend with here. Instead, He says believers should give greater concern to daily spiritual clothing. In Colossians, He shares His fashion tips for an exceptional outfit that is sure to turn heads and will not absorb even one stain or be subject to any rips, tears, or holes.

> *Therefore, as God's chosen people, holy and dearly loved, clothe yourselves with compassion, kindness, humility, gentleness and patience. Bear with each other and forgive one another if any of you has a grievance against someone. Forgive as the Lord forgave you. And over all these virtues put on love, which binds them all together in perfect unity.*
>
> —COLOSSIANS 3:12–14

Tomorrow morning, I will be getting dressed with a whole new perspective!

CHAPTER 16

Removing the Monkeys

❧❧❧

ANYONE READING THIS SHOULD KNOW up front that I have a back problem. My condition resulted from my own poor judgment and take-charge nature; I attempted to stop a loaded bookshelf from falling in the school book room. I have been rewarded with a frequent reminder that I was not the heroine in this situation but rather the defeated who now has a bad back! My condition is manageable as long as I keep my exercise vertical—no more twisty-turny machines for me. I know if I stray from this, I will be out for the count—yes, flat on my back!

While this is an annoying condition I have learned to live with, I continue to have another type of back problem. Exercise doesn't seem to help, and it has taken me a while to get a handle on the treatment needed for this ailment. It seems to flare up, not when I am catching falling books, but rather when I am trying to catch falling people. Before I know it, I have a slew of monkeys riding on my back, each one representing a situation that I have convinced myself I am the only one who can bring resolve to. Over the years, I have learned the four principles that are quite effective for helping me remove the monkeys from my back. That is a good thing, since the average spider monkey weighs approximately sixty pounds! If you secretly or openly suffer from this "back condition," read on to remove the monkeys.

MONKEY 1: HOWLING MONKEYS

Problems are inevitable! When I step outside my front door, problems are always there waiting to meet me. Though I try to escape them, they show up everywhere, infiltrating my workplace, church, favorite shopping spot (particularly at those half-off sales in the shoe department), and even in the market where I shop (especially during "piranha hour" right after work). When problems are all around me, it is good to be reminded that I am *not* responsible for always taking them on…empathizing and even sympathizing at times, but taking them as my own? Not always.

Some years ago, I learned this truth, and not vicariously. I seem to have a sign, invisible to me but visible to everyone else, that reads "*Tell me your problems. I am here to listen.*" I found myself repeatedly being the sounding board for a particular employee at work. This person operated on one level of emotion—full-blown. Disappointments were equal to disasters. Patiently, I would listen, try to console, and find myself committing to help find a solution, and that is exactly what I would do. When I would return the next day with solutions in hand, my colleague would almost never mention the situation I labored so long over without my prompting. I came to realize it was I who had the problem! Knowing when someone wanted a listener and when he or she wanted a problem solver was not a skill I had yet mastered.

- **Lesson Learned:** Every problem brought to my attention is worthy of my attention, concern, and prayer, but it is not always mine to take on personally.
- **Action to Take:** Remove the monkey.

Monkey 2: The Futility of Swinging in Someone Else's Tree

For seven years I gave up my classroom and stayed at home with our two girls. While I am grateful for that opportunity, there were times I felt a little less than fulfilled (I am a workaholic). So I was very flattered when a friend took note of my organizational skills and asked me to organize her home as well. Early one morning, I dropped the girls off to spend the day with friends at our Mother's Day Out program and promptly went over to do my organizing magic. It wasn't long before I realized that I was there not to teach my friend how to prevent this problem in the future but rather to clean up the current problem. While the work was accomplished, the skills I had hoped to teach were not conveyed or even asked for. Returning home that night, I looked at the disarray left in my own house that day to go swing in another tree and decided that next time—if given a next time—I would listen closely to what I was being asked to do.

- ❖ **Lesson Learned:** Listen, be slow to speak, and offer wise counsel—not free labor, unless that was your intent from the beginning.
- ❖ **Action to Take:** Remove the monkey.

Monkey 3: Peeling Everyone's Bananas Equals Overload

Doing everything for everyone doesn't make you the leader of a task. It simply makes you the load bearer. Running around doing this instead of sharing the load places the recipients of your efforts in charge of you! Several years ago while working on an initiative at my job, I purposed in my heart that I would make this as painless and palatable as possible. I labored for hours on preparation, presentation, and delivery, only to have sharp criticism shot my way followed by resistance, balking, and strain. Naturally I was offended, but in hindsight, why should I have been so surprised? I was the only one making the effort to pull this off. There was no buy-in, no ownership, no personal cost or effort involved. Therefore, all my work meant nothing to anyone except me.

- ❖ **Lesson Learned:** Leading does not mean doing everything for everyone, for in doing so you relinquish your leadership and become the workhorse of many sometimes ungrateful, or at the very least unhappy, recipients.
- ❖ **Action to Take:** Remove the monkey.

Monkey 4: Identifying and Empowering Troop Leaders

Monkeys live and travel in troops and are usually led by the most dominant male. While your employees, colleagues, or fellow club members are not monkeys (although they may act like them sometimes), it is wise when trying to remove the monkeys from your back to recognize that you are not the only one who can lead. Look for emerging leadership qualities in the circles you travel within. By training others, you can greatly reduce unnecessary workload. Building capacity in others will strengthen an organization and provide you with the satisfaction that you helped (not single-handedly accomplished) establish such a lasting effort.

* **Lesson Learned**
* **Action to Take:** Remove the monkey.

The Bible is very clear about our responsibility to carry the burdens of others, namely those of fellow believers. However, it does not say that we are to do this by having a "save the world," prideful attitude and belief that it is all up to us. Rather it says that burdens, loads, and cares are to be shared. This may mean different things in different situations. We need only to be sensitive to the Spirit of God as we encounter others and allow Him to lead us in the way we should go. I am confident he never intended us to carry one another's burdens *and* a load of monkeys!

Carry each other's burdens, and in this way
you will fulfill the law of Christ.

—*Galatians 6:2*

CHAPTER 17

Praying Through Your Pandora's Box

MYTHOLOGY HAS NEVER BEEN ONE of my literature loves. I loathed the units in both high school and college days that forced me to read selections or in some cases entire books that for me were nothing more than pure absurdity. How could heavenly creatures manifested in the form of gods and goddesses or the roaming of lowly demons of the underworld upon the earth have anything to do with reality? What was the point of these stories? With little life experience under my belt, I saw no correlation. At their best, these stories were merely unrealistic.

Much later in life, I have to admit, I still didn't gravitate to mythology; however, I did remember some of the ancient stories. For the first time, I saw some purpose for these writings. Like Pandora, I too had my own box of woes. While hers was indicative of the evils that would be spread throughout the world were she to open her box (and she did), mine was a little more personal. Inside my box, every hurt, disappointment, betrayal, grudge, and concern that I had ever had were not found, but rather my box included those I had never brought to the throne room of my Father.

So on an appointed day, worn down and feeling weak, and against my better human judgment, I did it...I opened the box. It had been closed so long that I was certain I would not withstand the pain my spirit would soon be experiencing, but at this point, there was no turning back. That day, I recited to the Lord the contents of my box. I knew I had no choice but to call them what they really were—despair, confusion, indifference, guilt, shame, and even hopelessness. Because I had squelched my release of these for so long, I had to add pride and bitterness to the list. There was really no blame game to play that day...no reason to look for who was at fault. What really mattered at this point was the decision to deal with them—yes, *all* of them. I didn't use formal language or format in my prayer. I'm not even sure I spoke in complete sentences. But I did release the hindering contents for the chance to start again.

Every problem was not solved that day; every prayer was not answered. Injustices were still at large and always will be. But for the first time in a long time, I found *hope* for working through these issues. It seemed to be hidden and sort of flattened and disheveled in the bottom of my box, yet it was making every effort to reshape and position itself once again near the top of the box after being suppressed for so long. I wondered why I needed to get to such a desperate point, and I concluded that it was because it allowed me to see my great need for Him—all of Him—in every part of my life.

Cast all your anxiety on him because he cares for you.

—*1 Peter 5:7*

CHAPTER 18

The Miracle of Hymns

❧

Whosoever Shorty-Minter-Me,
Shorty-Minter Me
Oh Shorty Minter Me,
Whosoever Shorty Minter Me,
Whosoever will may come!

THESE WERE MY WORDS MORE than forty years ago when I decided as a five-year-old to sing with all the gusto I could muster the old hymn "Whosoever Meaneth Me." Shorty Minter was our music minister at the time, and I was certain this song was all about him. I liked Shorty and his wife, Vera, very much and visited in their home on occasion, so I wanted to do the song complete justice. To this day, when I hear this old song I still laugh aloud, as it has as its markings the beginning of my love for the hymns of the church.

As far back as I can remember, my mother was always the church accompanist, whether she was playing the piano or the organ. She took us to church faithfully when we were children, so I spent a lot of years sitting on the second-row pew under her watchful eyes while she played for the congregation. Sometimes her eyes met mine with approval, and at other times I knew it was time to change my mind about my present behavior while occupying that pew unattended. Until I experienced motherhood myself, I had no idea how she could convey such an effective message of her expectations for my behavior. She did so seamlessly, without a word and without ever missing a note! I am thankful she remained a constant in my early years. I not only learned to sing hymns, but I also learned to play them on the piano. Later, such songs followed me into youth choir, playing at the local retirement home as a teenager, and even teaching children's choir as a young adult. Little did I realize then how tightly the truths of the lyrics written so long ago would be woven into the tapestry of my personal faith. Through the years, they have been a timeless source of the certainty of God's presence, affirmation, and blessings, and at times, great comfort.

The miracle of hymns is that each one has a story of its own, and the hymns are written by real people who experienced despair, disappointment, confusion, conviction, grief, joy, hope, and amazement just as we do today. They have a way of penetrating our hearts with exactly the right measure of strength and assurance we need at any given moment. Hymns uncover joy that has been suppressed and at times hidden by the cares of this world. Amazingly, they have stood the test of time and still flourish today, whether in traditional or contemporary form, and they minister in so many ways if we will but open our hearts.

Today I am proclaiming gratitude for a mother who, whether she knew it as a young parent or not, showed me the importance of worship, not only in prayer and scripture, but also in the singing of songs to the Lord.

Therefore I will praise you, Lord, among the nations;
I will sing the praises of your name.

—*Psalm 18:49*

CHAPTER 19

Cloudy with a Chance of Cheese Enchiladas

WHEN IT COMES TO CHEESE enchiladas, chips, and hot sauce, I suddenly become directionally challenged. I can quickly change whatever course I am currently on (including diets) just to get to my most favorite foods in the world! More often than not, I would have been wise to take a few hints from my stomach not to eat them too late at night, for this can produce hours of insomnia followed by crazy dreams and the need for a half roll of antacids. If my stomach could speak, it would simply say, "Do not do this again!" Simple enough to follow—if I just would!

Finding direction for life, especially spiritual direction, is a difficult matter. Choosing which way to go is like late-night enchiladas: some possibilities are obviously not good ones, but others are a bit more ambiguous. Therein lies the "maybe so...maybe not" seesaw of thinking when trying to decide. How do you really know what direction to take? How can you be sure that God is directing your steps?

Wouldn't it be great if you could just say, "God, if you will tell me exactly what to do, I will do it?" Sounds simple enough, and God could do just that! However, He rarely chooses to reveal His direction in that way. Why is that? I imagine Him responding something like this:

My Child,
I have given specific directions before...think about Abraham. I told him that
he would have a son at the appointed time. Consider Moses. All that I asked of
him was to speak on behalf of the children of Israel before the pharaoh. Finally,

remember Jonah? I asked him to go to Nineveh to let the people know I would save them if they would only repent. Tell me which of the three complied with my directions? You would be right if you said none. Instead, Abraham took matters into his own hands, Moses argued with me about his ability to speak, and Jonah ran in the opposite direction. The thing is…since I made you just like I made these men, I know what you will do. Therefore, I want you to be a seeker of my will. That's right, a seeker.

Your Father, God

Considerations for the Spiritually Directionally Challenged

Is what I am planning to do, or where I am planning to go, in agreement with the context of scripture?

I have chosen the way of faithfulness; I have set my heart on your laws.

—PSALM 119:30

Is this direction the result of a heartfelt desire that has been resurfacing in my spirit and in my prayer life?

But those who live in accordance with the Spirit have
their minds set on what the Spirit desires.

—ROMANS 8:5

Will this direction help me to help others know Christ?

I will give them a heart to know me, that I am the LORD.
They will be my people and I will be their God.

—JEREMIAH 24:7

Am I willing to give up possessions, prestige and any other deterrent to follow?

For everything in the world—the lust of the flesh, the lust of the eyes,
and the pride of life—comes not from the Father but from the world.

—*1 John 2:16*

Would I be willing to go another direction if God changed my course? Which is more important: my desires or God's desires accomplished through me?

Many are the plans in a person's heart, but it is
the Lord's purpose that prevails.

—*Proverbs 19:21*

Will following this direction have eternal value?

His ways are eternal.

—*Habakkuk 3:6*

Direct me in the path of your commands,
for there I find delight.
Turn my heart toward your statutes
and not toward selfish gain.
Turn my eyes away from worthless things;
preserve my life according to your word.

—*Psalm 119:35–37*

Time Marches On

WEDDINGS ARE LOVELY OCCASIONS, AS they bestow a certain measure of joyfulness and anticipation along with a reminder that, with this beginning, a love is born that is new, hopeful, and untethered by the storms of life. For that instant, it seems the moment will last forever. Weddings establish a "we" and wave fare-well to a "me" way of thinking. A wedding is the beginning of a life story.

Memorials are also commemorative, but instead of beginnings they focus on earthly endings—the culmination of a life story. They bring about the relin-quishing of the "we" and the return to "me." Recently, I experienced both types of occasions in the same week, and I was reminded of how quickly life passes by. *What is it that transports us from a youthful bride or bridegroom to one who is feeling the creeping of age in seemingly the blink of an eye?*

Time. It's is the medium that the experiences of life travel through. As it marches on, time is indifferent to happenings along the pathway of life. It pays no attention to the ups and downs and never notices when there is soaring through joyous times or when there is trudging through sorrows that leave one barely hanging on. It lacks understanding of efforts made to hold to commit-ment, and it doesn't see those sacrificial investments that make the life story a rich one. Instead it keeps a steady cadence and marches on until the final life chapter is written.

Whether you are at the beginning, the end, or maybe somewhere in the middle of your own life story, there are many beginnings, middles, and end-ings throughout the journey. While time is indifferent, God is not. He says our times—all of them—are in His hands! He is the conductor who orchestrates,

He is the sculptor who shapes, and He is the anchor who holds us together through every experience and every season of our life story.

> *There is a time for everything,*
> *and a season for every activity under the heavens:*
> *a time to be born and a time to die,*
> *a time to plant a time to uproot,*
> *a time to kill and a time to heal,*
> *a time to tear down and a time to build,*
> *a time to weep and a time to laugh,*
> *a time to mourn and a time to dance,*
> *a time to scatter stones and a time to gather them,*
> *a time to embrace and a time to refrain from embracing,*
> *a time to search and a time to give up,*
> *a time to keep and a time to throw away,*
> *a time to tear and a time to mend,*
> *a time to be silent and a time to speak,*
> *a time to love and a time to hate,*
> *a time for war and a time for peace.*
>
> —*ECCLESIASTES 3:1–8*

> *He has also set eternity in the hearts of men: yet they cannot*
> *fathom what God has done from beginning to end.*
>
> —*ECCLESIASTES 3:11*

CHAPTER 21

Christian Chameleons

We are like chameleons. We take our hue and the color of
our moral character from those who are around us.

—JOHN LOCKE

I CERTAINLY IDENTIFY WITH THE title character in Eric Carle's book *The Mixed-Up Chameleon*. It's the story of a young chameleon who just wanted to be like everyone else. So on a particular day, unsatisfied with who he was, he took on the likeness of every animal he met. Satisfied for a while, he later realized he had assumed the characteristics of so many different animals that he could no longer find himself.

As believers in Jesus Christ, isn't that our story at times? We come to believe that it is permissible for something or someone other than God to shape our character. In doing so, we become *Christian chameleons* and compromise our convictions for comfort—just to be like the rest of the world. Staying true to our beliefs is tough to do! The world cries out to us through media, music, literature, and even people we consistently come in contact with that we need to change, to get with the times, to be more tolerant, and to justify that what society says is acceptable indeed is.

Adopting the world's message is an almost certain way to not be in sync with God's word. Standing for truth is like a wrestling match played out between truth and falsehood. The fight is not a quick one but rather a slow fading of values that once produced strong conviction. It's an erosion of a heart that was once in tune, a crossing over the line. Its indifference is brought on by the hard knocks of life and the notion that decides that giving in is less painful. And without caution, the white flag of surrender is waved and truth is pulled across the victory line, both defeated and burdened because there has been compromise. Before we know it, like the Mixed-Up Chameleon, we no longer know who we are or what we stand for.

In the book of Corinthians 15–16, the word of God reminds us that this is not a new problem but rather an age-old one. The early Christians of Corinth, like us, battled ideals, practices, and beliefs that did not align with the word of God. God's answer to what we should do was the same then and now. It is timeless.

> *Be on your guard, stand firm in the faith; be*
> *courageous; be strong. Do everything in love.*
>
> —1 CORINTHIANS 16:13

> *Therefore my dear brothers and sisters, stand firm. Let nothing*
> *move you. Always give yourselves fully to the work of the Lord,*
> *because you know that your labor in the Lord is not in vain.*
>
> —1 CORINTHIANS 15:58

Father,
Please guard my eyes that I may not take them off truth.
Guard my ears that I may discern the intent of messages given to me by others.
Guard my mouth that I may not use words that hurt but rather heal.
Guard my mind that I may keep pure thoughts and sound reason.
Guard my heart so that I may always be attentive to your direction.
Amen

CHAPTER 22

Tackling Temptation

⌘

JUST WHEN YOU THINK YOU'VE got everything in your life balanced, "it" happens. You really don't want to go there, but you feel compelled. Though your spirit is a little unsettled, you entertain the possibilities that arise from a mere thought, suggestion, or opportunity. Without careful watch, you can find yourself tipping the scales of your life in the unfavorable direction of temptation.

Not too long ago, after struggling with a hard decision in my own life, I asked a friend to please tell me the greatest struggle in her life. Why I did this, I do not know. I would not want to air my greatest temptations. They seem to be a private matter. Nevertheless, I asked. Feeling a little invasive, I waited awkwardly. After a few seconds, she responded, "I am not sure what the greatest temptation is. I have so many." The honesty of this friend spoke volumes to me about where most of us are in life with our struggles. Many choose to suffer in silence. They view God as an angry judge waiting to strike down the gavel on them and all the while try to outwardly appear like they have life together. There's never a time when they come to grips with their temptations, and therefore they continue to feel judged, defeated, and hopeless about the possibility of ever resolving the struggles they are facing. They go on and on with no victory—only defeat.

We do not have to look much past ourselves to find others who have suffered from temptations. The truth is they are present in people everywhere—work, school, church, civic clubs, and in lines at the market and post office. Virtually everywhere. The Bible is full of stories of God's people—yes, followers—who suffered from temptation. The outcomes were sometimes triumphant and sometimes tragic. So why should you or I think we are any different? How can we conquer this robber of peace? What does it take to restore the joy and contentment that temptation can take from our lives and our relationships with others?

RECOGNIZE

Everyone is tempted. Yes, that's right. If you are in an earth suit, you will suffer from temptation in some form, regardless of your spiritual strength or position, or lack thereof. This is no surprise to God!

Acknowledge it! God needs no sugarcoated prayers. No excuses! No rationalizations! No suppressing the temptation! Speak with your Heavenly Father, and call it what it is: temptation.

No temptation has overtaken you except what is common to mankind.

—*1 CORINTHIANS 10:13*

REFUSE SELF-RELIANCE

Do not try to get past temptation on your own. It won't happen! Wonder why? Satan knows our "bent to sin." He studies us, waits for the right situation, and uses our weaknesses against us every time.

Admit you are weak in your own strength. Run to God—not away from Him.

Watch and pray so that you will not fall into temptation,
the spirit is willing but the flesh is weak.

—*MATTHEW 26:41*

REFUTE THE ENEMY

You have to make a choice. Either you act on your temptation, or you refute it! There's no middle ground. Acting on your temptation crosses the line, and the Bible refers to this as sin.

Walk away if necessary. Bring your thoughts, suggestions made, and opportunities offered captive to Christ.

Then, after desire has conceived, it gives birth to sin; and
sin, when it is full-grown, gives birth to death.

—James 1:15

Remember the Promise

Since temptation is nothing new to God (remember, Jesus had a pretty grueling experience with Satan's temptation tactics Himself), He reminds us that He always provides a way out. We can bear consequences, or we can conquer them!

And God is faithful; he will not let you be tempted beyond
what you can bear. But when you are tempted, he will
also provide a way out so that you can endure it.

—1 Corinthians 10:13

Receive the Reward

Overcoming temptation carries with it great rewards. Faithfulness on our parts can reap great blessings in our own lives and the lives of others.

Blessed is the man who perseveres under trial, because when he has stood the
test, he will receive the crown of life that God promised to those who love Him.

—James 1:12

Dear God,
Thank you that I can bring every struggle, temptation, and trial to you with
no fear of your rejection. I am grateful that simple admittance that I need your

help in a matter is sufficient. I rest in the fact that there is nothing too large or small for you to attend to, and I find my strength to overcome my challenges in you alone. Thank you for offering to me the strength to be a conqueror through your power in me.
Amen

CHAPTER 23

Rahab: Point Woman for God

SHE WAS JERICHO'S "LADY OF the night." The Bible refers to her as a harlot. Some say she ran an inn there, and others believe it really was nothing more than a brothel. Regardless, it was the place the men of the city gathered to trade stories and get in on the latest gossip and scandals. Rahab was her name, and to most there she was all that she would ever be—a prostitute with a reputation that would precede her wherever she went for the rest of her days.

That is, until one day when two strangers entered the inn. She hadn't seen them around town before. The men, remaining as inconspicuous as possible, eavesdropped on the stories being swapped and spent no time conversing with the crowd. Rahab knew they must have some business in the city. Little did she know they were there to scout the town, to make notes on the layout of the city, and to size up how they would soon carry out their plan. Her thoughts were interrupted by a message from the king of Jericho. Rahab had often been a point person for the king. He relied on her to leak information when the city was threatened or possibly under attack. What better place was there than this hub visited by both locals and those traveling through? Surely the "two spies," as he called them, had been there. While Rahab realized these were the very men the king spoke of, she wrestled with disclosure. For some reason, this time was different.

These men were Israelites. The fear of them had spread rampantly throughout the city and to points beyond in the previous days. She had heard the reports of their intentions to take over the city. In fact, this was the very conversation she had heard among the men of the inn just that day. Right now, though, it was decision time. Dusk was falling, and she wondered if the men would ask for a room to stay the night or if they would venture out. Knowing that the king was in pursuit of the men, Rahab made a decision. This time she would not honor the king's request. She had heard the king's words. She knew what men of the city were speculating was about to happen, but she just couldn't sell them out. Some would accuse Rahab of treason, but in reality Rahab had come to the point of transformation.

She told the men to come with her because the king was pursuing them aggressively and soon they would be found if she did not hide them. The men agreed, and she hid them on her rooftop under flax that she had been storing there. Before the night was over, Rahab approached the men and confessed that their God was the one true God. She said he was the God of the heaven above and earth below. Earnestly, she explained how fearful the people of the city were of this very happening that was about to come to pass and asked the men to save her family from the desolation that was quickly approaching. The men could clearly see her predicament. She had not honored the king's request but rather had become a point person to help them carry out their plan. This decision could only mean one thing for her—destruction, be it from the king or through the invasion. She had risked it all to help these men accomplish the plan God had laid before them.

That night an agreement was made that a scarlet cord would be hung in the window of Rahab's home. It was hung in the window, first as a reminder that Rahab and her family were to be saved during the siege for her faithfulness to God and also as a foreshadowing of the redeeming power of Christ that was to come through His birth, death, and resurrection. Rahab continued to live with the Israelites and became the mother of Boaz, from which the lineage of Jesus Christ came.

The concept of the "point man" is interesting to me. It refers to one who helps to carry out an endeavor or job. The Bible is full of point men and women who fulfilled God's assignments throughout history, but what about today? Most likely you and I both have friends, family, and loved ones who desperately need a point man/woman to intervene in their lives. The reasons they need help are varied, but ultimately they need someone to guide them, encourage them, and be that one who sees them through. I am sure Rahab had no idea that she would be the one to share in the lineage of Jesus Christ himself, but God saw her from a very different perspective. So it is with us. Therefore, we should not grow weary when we do not see change as quickly as we like in those we are deeply concerned about, whatever the reason might be. Rather, we must pray for the point man or woman God will send, remembering that God will do the choosing, not us. He will identify the qualities needed in the point people he uses, and as God often does, He will use individuals you and I have judged, deemed not qualified, or—if I dare say—pronounced unworthy. At the appointed time, He will bring about the finished work of Christ in our lives and in the lives of our loved ones, and we will be amazed at how He chooses to do it!

> *By faith the walls of Jericho fell, after the army had marched around them for seven days. By faith the prostitute Rahab, because she welcomed the spies, was not killed with those who were disobedient.*
>
> —*Hebrews 11:30–31*

Speechless

Always preach the gospel; when necessary, use words.

—Unknown

IT WAS TIME FOR THE monthly visit to the obstetrician. We were expecting our second child in a few months, and I was thoughtfully making a list of the questions I wanted to ask my doctor. When I arrived, I found that I would be seeing his partner that day. Though I preferred the convenience and comfort of seeing someone I knew, I was fine with the change. Mentally, though, I worried that he wouldn't be a "question answering" kind of doctor and I would leave the visit with my questions answered. We spent the first few minutes with me responding to his routine questions and hearing about what to expect in the future. As it happened, I did get my questions answered, and as the visit was drawing to a close, he suddenly said, "I have one more question." I felt a sharp streak of fear go through me. I waited expectantly, dreading what he might say next. Was something wrong that he had just picked up on in our conversation? I can't remember his exact words, but in paraphrase he said, "Tell me, what is different about you? You have a peace I have not seen in others."

At this, I just about fell out of the chair. My mind was racing. I had not come with my heart prepared to have this type of conversation. I am sure I looked rather surprised, but I managed to say something that pointed him to the fact that I was a believer. I left the office numb and speechless. I didn't share this experience with others. I just wanted to ponder it for a while. I wanted to grasp the importance of what God was teaching me. Replaying the conversation on the way home, I thought, *This question came out of nowhere.* Really, though, it hadn't. It was God's reminder to me that I always have to be on alert, sensitive to those opportunities that require not only living my life as an example of Christ within me but also sharing Christ through words. While actions are sometimes enough to draw people to Him, other times words are needed. Today was definitely a day that had called for words.

I did not see that doctor again during my pregnancy. One Sunday, several years later, I recognized him walking down the aisle of our church during the altar call. He had his wife with him. Soon after, they were both baptized into the church. Later, I had the privilege of teaching one of his grandchildren, and in recent years, I had the opportunity to hear one of his own children speak about missionary work he was doing in another country.

Whatever awkward words I answered this man with that day in the doctor's office, I know God used them. Today, I still rejoice every time I see him. I am sure he doesn't remember me, but I remember him. I thank God for taking my disheveled, unprepared response and using it as a small part in directing him to Christ. So as I pass by him, I just smile and silently say, *Thank you.*

> *Always be prepared to give an answer to everyone who asks you to give the reason for the hope that you have. But do so with gentleness and respect.*
>
> —1 Peter 3:15

Password Problems

MY PASSWORD PROBLEM IS SIMPLE: I have too many of them. The digital age has brought me a lot of convenience in most areas of life—except for passwords. I have some for work, some for play, and others to make sure the bills get paid. However, and more often than I care to admit, I find myself visiting the "change your password" site because I tend to forget them. I've tried many methods. I've used one for everything, but that's not safe. I've tried creating a password with an association or something related—that was a fiasco. And finally, I resorted to an ancient method…pen and paper. I decided that one small piece of paper, easily folded and tucked away in a secret place, would solve my problems with passwords. And it did—until I discovered I had too many for the page. Once again, the possibility of solving this problem grew dim. My paper resembled a jumbled mess! Needed organization was quite apparent, and so I did what any other "trying to get organized" person would do and got a planner that had specially designated pages for usernames and passwords. Carefully I wrote them all in their appointed spaces under the correct categories and felt such satisfaction at the completion of this project. The online world was once again at my fingertips! Or was it?

I got to the meeting just in time to slide into one of the two last available seats in the back of the room. The presenter had already started, so I tried to be as inconspicuous as possible. After all, no one needed to know I had actually been on time to this meeting but just at the wrong location! Anyway, I attempted to settle myself and get busy following the directions to open my device to a particular website. *No sweat,* I thought to myself. I had just been there a few days before with no problems and decided this day was going to turn out all right after all. However, as I attempted to log on, I got that dreaded message we have all gotten from time to time: *Incorrect Password.* So I did what anyone would do, I tried it again and again and again until I realized I was going to get completely left behind if I didn't ask for help.

In my rush to get to the meeting on time, I had forgotten my planner with all my passwords inside. Reluctantly, I raised my hand, expecting someone to assist me with my dilemma so I could join the group, only to look around and discover that there were others in the same boat. The instructor quickly walked to the back corner of the room to visit with the PWP (people without passwords) group, and with a semisweet, semisour demeanor she began to expound on the importance of remembering our passwords. At this point, I wanted nothing more than to crawl into a shell or even just a dark corner in the room, as her voice level and intent was such that everyone in the room would be privy to her disappointment with us, the PWPs. No matter what I tried from memory, nothing would work. The instructor claimed that I did not have an account set up. Though I knew that to be untrue, insisting that I did have one would not resolve the problem. I was at the point where I couldn't help myself any longer, so I cried *uncle* to the lecture of forgetting my password and walked to the front of the room, certain I was hearing the "Death March" playing in the background, to set up a new account…yes, in front of everyone! I wrote this password down.

While forgetting my password that day made me feel embarrassed and viewed as not responsible, I knew the truth about myself. I am a responsible person. I will probably continue to forget passwords from time to time. That day I decided that at this point in life, I should concentrate on remembering the password book rather than each password.

The book of Acts tells the story of the Philippian jailer who guarded Paul and Silas when they were thrown into a Roman prison and placed in shackles. Their constant singing of praises to God lulled the jailer into a sweet slumber— that was, until a terrifying earthquake shook the entire jail, loosened the shackles from the prisoners, and awakened the jailer. How would he ever explain going to sleep while on watch? Knowing the outcome was dim, the jailer drew his sword and decided to take his own life. There was no one who could save him from his defeat, so he thought he might as well end it all now. Suddenly, he heard Paul cry out, "Don't harm yourself. We are all here!" At this, the jailer put away his sword. His mind returned to the songs he had heard earlier of praise to God. He knew he needed what these men had. At that point, Paul delivered a single word that could save the both the physical and spiritual life of the jailer. He simply said, "Believe." No great heroic deeds, no flowery prayers that showered the listeners with abundance of words, no expensive offerings needed—just *believe*. This was a "password" of sorts, unlike any the man had previously heard as he guarded the prison cells.

The story closes with the jailer and his whole family coming to faith in Christ. Paul and Silas's stop at the Roman prison was for a distinct reason: to deliver the password needed by both the jailer then and all humankind both then and now...*believe*.

Dear God,

My password book is reflective of my earthly accounts. Sometimes I am forgetful, and I acknowledge I need it while I am here on this earth. However, I also know these words are temporal, useful for this season of my life. Right now, though, I want to reflect on the timeless password you have already revealed to me, one that has opened the door to eternity even before I need it. It is believe. *Just that simple. I really don't need to write this one down, for it is already imprinted on my heart. For the Bible says in Acts 16:31: "Believe in the Lord Jesus Christ, and you will be saved, you and your household."*

A CHRISTmas Story: It's about Two Trees

◈

I never thought it was such a bad little tree. It's not bad
at all, really. Maybe it just needs a little love.

—LINUS VAN PELT

OVER THE YEARS, MY CHRISTMAS tree has become quite the conversation piece. Behind everything that bears such uniqueness is a great story waiting to be told, so here is mine. When my husband and I married almost twenty-six years ago, as couples usually do, we merged our belongings. One of the things I brought with me was my beautiful Christmas tree. I had purchased it several years before and was so proud of the stature and beauty it graced my living room with each holiday season as I placed it in front of the window. Having been a bachelor for thirty-two years, my husband did not own a tree and had no objection to mine becoming the family tree. For several years, the tree took its usual place in the living room window, though in a new home.

This placement of the tree continued until our oldest daughter was a little over a year old. My husband, who has always been an excellent safety monitor, was worried about putting the Christmas tree in its usual place. While he had some valid points about what could happen—such as our daughter pulling the tree over on her or eating the tinsel or breaking the ornaments and hurting herself—I was a stay-at-home mom and kept a watchful eye on her every day. I was confident I could prevent any of these things from happening. After much discussion about what we should do with the tree, we never resolved the issue. That's correct. *We* never resolved the issue.

One December afternoon, I returned home from Christmas shopping to find the Christmas tree standing upright on the dining room table—yes, *on the table*. While this seemed odd, something wasn't quite the same. What was different besides the location? Suddenly, I realized the tree was much shorter! After studying the tree for a minute, I discovered that the middle section had disappeared. Hubby had taken his hacksaw and cut the tree in half, removing about two feet off the bottom section. Why would he do such a foolish thing? He was so proud, as it solved our safety problem, but to me it was no longer pretty and looked a little malformed. It appeared I now had officially become the owner of a Charlie Brown Christmas tree, and there was no one else to blame besides Mr. Safety himself. Although I was none too happy with this situation, my mother was visiting, and the last thing I wanted was to lose my cool with my husband in front of her, so I agreed we would have Christmas this year with this odd-looking version of a tree. I vowed to myself that we would have a new tree next year and it would take its rightful place in the living room window.

Good intentions are always admirable, but one year turned into two and so on, until we had placed this little tree in our living room for twenty-four years. I always intended to buy a new one, but year after year I grew more attached to it. The uneven branches, some too big and some too small for its trunk, held mementos that told *our story*, including how it came to be a *little Christmas tree*. At nighttime, when everyone was asleep, I would relish the time spent with the lights out and the tree lit up. The girls' homemade ornaments, as well as gifts given to me by students, glistened in the light, and I was reminded again of how thankful I am for the life I have been given and the family I have to share it with.

My children are adults now, and under great peer pressure I was encouraged once again to buy a new tree. So I did, and this year we will place it in the spot the other tree occupied for so long. However, though it will be a vision of loveliness and will be beautifully decorated, I am waiting to see if my children will miss the old tree as much as I will. (And just in case they do, it will be waiting in another room ready to remind them of our wonderful memories held in its branches.)

While it seemed foolish to me, and I was the foolish one, altering the tree was my husband's way of saving my daughter from herself. Long ago, there was another tree. It was carefully created, nourished, and loved by its creator. This tree, though a thing of beauty at one time, was created for a purpose unlike any others of its kind. It was not made to bear fruit or to be shade from the noonday heat. It was not designed as a resting spot for a weary traveler or a home for the birds of the air. Its very resolve was to be the instrument that would save sinful humankind from itself. This tree too was altered—stripped of its beautiful branches and uprooted from the place it flourished to be made into the wooden cross upon which Jesus Christ, the Son of God, died to provide eternal life for all who will believe. The cross has become a bridge for every person who once thought he could find his own way to God, and it has become the emblem of the power of God in the lives of those who willingly choose to believe.

> *For the message of the cross is foolishness to those who are perishing,*
> *but to us who are being saved it is the power of God.*

> —*1 Corinthians 1:18*

CHAPTER 27

Lessons from Broken Things

My sixteenth birthday was a milestone in my life. I thought this was because now I was able to get my first job, drive a car, and go on my first date. I had looked forward to that day for a long time. Indeed, it was a milestone, but not so much for the reasons I had expected. Rather, it was a birthday that set the stage to teach me one of the most valuable lessons of my life.

My parents owned a small business that was very dependent on the oil industry, and about the time of my sixteenth birthday, it plummeted to an all-time low. In fact, the economy was so bad at that time that my dad had to close his doors for a few months and work another job until the market settled and he could afford to reopen. Times were very tough financially, but I was unaware of this because my parents worked as hard as they possibly could to not let it affect us in any way.

On the day of my birthday, we did the usual routine. My mom made a cake, happy-birthday hooplas were said and sung, and then it was present time. Since this was my sixteenth, I wondered if this would be an extra-special present. I looked at the package and wondered what could possibly be in the box. My mind was wild with imagination. *Keys to a new car? Mega shopping trip? Jewelry?* When I opened the package, my anticipation suddenly turned to disappointment. I quickly realized the need to continue my excited disposition and not let my countenance drop. The last thing I ever wanted to do was to hurt my parents' feelings. Inside the package there was no set of keys, no cash for a shopping trip, and no jewelry. Instead, inside I found a jewelry box. Though it was beautifully carved from wood in a free-form style that looked somewhat like a puzzle, it was not at all what I had expected nor what I had wanted. I was ashamed of myself, but I was disappointed.

I kept the jewelry box on my dresser for the rest of the time I lived in my parents' house, and I took it with me to college and later to my own home. At some point in a move, it was broken, but I could not bring myself to throw it away. Instead, I put the pieces in a box and moved the box each time I moved. You see, this jewelry box proved to be quite a lesson for me. It was the beginning of my understanding of the proper placement of expectations. That day so long ago, my parents had given me their best. The disappointment I felt was not their fault but mine. I had placed expectations on them that they simply could not meet at that time. If that wasn't bad enough, I let their lack of meeting my expectations turn me into a disappointed person. It had been all about me and what *they* could do to make me happy.

Expectations are important to have in life. We set them in our jobs, in our relationships, in resolving health issues, and when setting goals and defining our dreams. So why do we sometimes find ourselves in a state of disappointment regarding them? Simply said, expectations were never meant to be held out as something that is certain or guaranteed. By their very definition, expectations are simply what we expect or look forward to happening.

I think the Bible suggests we trade in the word *expectations* for a word that has more surety attached to it. That word is *hope*. The Bible refers to hope as an "anchor for our souls." Regardless of the economy or any other man-made disaster or failure that may tempt us with disappointment, we can know that hope always stands firm. Broken and useless now, the pieces of the jewelry box stand as a reminder of the precious truth I learned. I would not trade the contents of that box for all the new cars, shopping trips, or jewelry in the world. I now understand that one thing will never disappoint, and that one thing is hope.

Put your hope in God.

—*Psalm 42:5*

We have this hope as an anchor for the soul, firm and secure.

—*Hebrews 6:19*

And hope does not disappoint us.

—*Romans 5:5*

CHAPTER 28

The Power of Words: Ten Truths about Them

"STICKS AND STONES MAY BREAK my bones, but words will never hurt me!" As a primary teacher, I heard this quite often, just as when I was a child, I'm sure I said it myself. There is something within all of us that tends to rise up and fan a desire to lash out when we are offended by another. If we do not stop and think before we speak, we will use the one weapon powerful enough to avenge our enemy—our words.

I would like to say I have only been on the receiving end of unkind words, but in reality there have been times I have been on the giving end as well. Try as I may, under just the right stressful circumstances those words just begin to slip out, and before I know it, I have said enough to regret ever saying anything at all! How I desire the discipline to routinely recognize the power of my words and mindfully choose them more carefully.

The scriptures provide us with some insightful truths concerning the influence our words, both kind and unkind, can have on others. It also confirms the potential they have to affect others positively or negatively.

10 TRUTHS ABOUT WORDS

1.   Words have the power to extinguish anger or ignite it.

> *A gentle answer turns away wrath, but a harsh word stirs up anger.*

> —*PROVERBS 15:1*

2. Words recklessly spoken can break the heart and spirit of someone.

    The words of the reckless pierce like a sword, but
    the tongue of the wise brings healing.

    —PROVERBS *12:18*

3. Words paint a lasting impression, whether it is good or bad, in the eye of another.

    The words of a gossip are like choice morsels;
    they go down to the inmost parts.

    —PROVERBS *26:22*

4. Words can exhaust and annoy the listener.

    A quarrelsome wife is like the dripping of a leaky roof in a rainstorm;
    restraining her is like restraining the wind or grasping oil with the hand.

    —PROVERBS *27:15*

5. Words unveil what is in the heart of a person.

    Make a tree good and its fruit will be good, or make a tree bad
    and its fruit will be bad, for a tree is recognized by its fruit.
    You brood of vipers, how can you who are evil say anything
    good? For the mouth speaks what the heart is full of.

    —MATTHEW *12:33–34*

6. Words can cause worry for someone or bring them cheer.

> *Anxiety weighs down the heart, but a kind word cheers it up.*
>
> —PROVERBS 12:2

7. Words of betrayal can bring distrust.

> *If you argue your case with a neighbor, do not betray another man's confidence,*
> *or he who hears it may shame you and you will never lose your bad reputation.*
>
> —PROVERBS 25:9–10

8. The right word spoken at the right time is custom-made by God for you.

> *A word aptly spoken is like apples of gold in settings of silver.*
>
> —PROVERBS 25:11

9. Words can provide eternal choices.

> *From this time many of his disciples turned back and no longer followed*
> *him. "You do not want to leave too, do you?" Jesus asked the Twelve. Simon*
> *Peter answered him, "Lord, to whom shall we go? You have the words of*
> *eternal life. We believe and know that you are the Holy One of God."*
>
> —JOHN 6:66–69

10. Words of the wise are grounded in biblical truth.

The words of the wise are like goads, their collected sayings
like firmly embedded nails—given by one shepherd.

—Ecclesiastes 12:11

Heavenly Father,
Give me words to say that are affirming, cheerful, wise, and timely. May I
remember that I hold the Word of Life in my heart. Help me through the words I
speak to share it with others.
Amen

Stuff: Don't Just Stuff It

Come to me all you who are weary and burdened, and I will give you rest. Take
my yoke upon you and learn from me, for I am gentle and humble in heart, and
you will find rest for your souls. For my yoke is easy and my burden is light.

—Matthew 11:28—30

She flinched as I introduced myself and gave her a firm handshake. In a matter of
seconds, I was informed that she had been badly beaten the night before.

Bending down to console a child who had stained her shirt, I learned that her
parent was incarcerated.

As I walked him down the hall, he informed me that he had had no water or
electricity for some time in his home.

Watching from nearby, I saw a youngster be taken by authorities, not to return home that evening.

THE SITUATIONS DESCRIBED ABOVE ARE few but representative of the "stuff" people are dealing with on a daily basis. Every day I see masses of people, but do I really "see" them? In all the busyness of the day, it is easy to be unaware or indifferent to the pain people are experiencing unless I consciously make the choice to ask God how I can be used by Him.

At some point, we all have situations or are aware of instances that seem hopeless. We may be tempted to think there is nothing we can do. We must remind ourselves of what the Bible says: with Christ, situations are never hopeless. Jesus speaks to this in Matthew 11:28–30. He gives two simple directives for us as needy people who come to Him on our own behalf or on the behalf of others.

First of all, Jesus says, "Come to me." Maybe you are like me in that your first thought, regardless of the magnitude of a problem you have or have witnessed, is "How do I fix this?" or "How do I control and maintain it?" Jesus says it so simply that it seems hard. Don't fix it. Don't control it. Just "Come to me." By coming to Jesus, we are acknowledging that we can no longer help ourselves or someone else in the situation, and we trust that He can. This enables us to quit being "silent sufferers" who bear the entire load of the problem. It releases us from having to have all the answers and hands it over to the One who *does* have the answers.

Secondly, Jesus tells us to "Take my yoke." This may seem like a somewhat foreign request for us today, but nevertheless, it is His directive. The yoke in biblical times was a harness that was placed across the backs of a team of animals to move a heavy load. As long as the animals worked together, submitting to the purpose of the harness, the load was lighter for everyone and the burden on their backs could be moved and the work accomplished. However, if one animal pulled against the yoke, great pain from the harness could be inflicted on all the animals and the work could not be completed. Likewise, when we take the spiritual yoke of Christ, we are allowing Him to place that spiritual harness across our backs and join Him in His work to move the burdens of life. As we submit to Him, we can experience His peace in the midst of the situation, and by patiently submitting, we can see His best unfold in the situation.

That is not to say that our burdens always go away immediately. Whether the solution comes quickly or takes time, Jesus promises to teach us and to give us rest and the ability to stand under the load, for it is now steered by the Master. He simply says, "Come to me."

CHAPTER 30

What's the Holdup, God? I'm Still Waiting

SOME SAY THERE ARE ONLY two things in life that are certain: death and taxes. While this clichéd statement is somewhat true, I believe that the span of time between birth and death should be named. What would it be called? *Waiting.* In every stage of life, we are always waiting for something or someone. As a child, waiting involved the Sears and Roebuck Christmas catalog, Christmas TV specials that aired only once a year, TV shows that if missed would not air again in a few days on the Internet, Saturday birthday parties, and report cards made from heavy cardstock that parents actually signed and returned.

As a teenager, waiting could be seen in such important events as an invitation to the homecoming dance or the hope that an unsightly blemish would disappear quickly. Waiting was evident in many things, such as finding out if you had been picked for the cheerleading squad, if you had passed your algebra test, and if you had gotten that perfect part-time job. Yes, waiting was still present, and it became more agonizing as time passed.

As a young adult, perhaps you remember waiting for your college degree to be conferred, for the thrill of your first real job, for your wedding day to arrive, and for the births of each of your children. As life kept happening, you became very familiar with waiting. It was always there to take its rightful place.

Forgive me for stating the obvious, but waiting is ever present in our lives! If, for some reason, waiting could speak, do you think it would announce, "You have had enough practice waiting, so I will be leaving now?" No! Instead it just continues right on making itself at home regardless of your season in life.

For me, wrestling with waiting was most difficult several years ago. My husband was diagnosed with a rare bone tumor. The local radiologist was concerned about the scans we thought were being done as the result of a sports injury, and instead he referred us to an oncologist who was a surgeon in this field. He wasn't sure what the diagnosis would be, but it didn't look too good. We were in shock, and the waiting for answers began. Soon after, we were able to see the oncologist. After more scans we learned that it was not identifiable yet and an operation should be performed as soon as possible. We were sent home to wait with no answers or direction. The following week, we returned for the surgery. The procedure lasted several hours. I waited prayerfully for good news. When the doctor conferred with me after surgery, he had no news. The rare tumor still had not been identifiable, had done extensive damage, and would have to be sent off for further research and identification. No indication was made as to whether or not it was malignant. So the waiting began again. Weeks passed before we received an answer. Thankfully, it was not malignant but was a very aggressive recurring tumor that could again do extensive damage if left unmonitored. We spent the next five years having annual checks to ensure it had not returned. We were so grateful after five years of waiting, yearly checks, and many prayers to learn that he was still tumor-free and would be released from the specialist.

In this situation—and many other ones as well—I have wanted to help God along so that the waiting process in a life event could be shorter and less painful. I began to notice that, when I've appointed myself during these times to help God out, He has been remotely silent and strangely distant in my life. Finally, when I have exhausted my efforts to hurry up change, He shows up, reminding me that there is no time travel to speed up His perfect will or plans.

It is embarrassing to say, but it has taken me almost half a century to discover that I have to do something different during the "waiting times" in my life. By act of my will, not always my heartfelt feelings at first, I invite God to make *His* desires for the request I am making to become *my* desires. My prayer is simple.

Lord, I want to be where you are in this. Wherever or whatever that may be, make that my desire.

After surrendering to waiting, it has been amazing to see how I am handling the waiting time in life's situations. Am I perfect at it? Have I arrived? Absolutely not! However, surrendering my will has brought peace, contentment, and joy that I know I will continue to have regardless of the outcome. Slowly, with some success, some failures, and much reminding, I am beginning to embrace waiting. It is both an adventure and anticipation, as I resolve that this time is much needed to change my desires to be a lot about Him and very little about me!

The promise of God concerning the "waiting times" in our lives says:

Do you not know?
Have you not heard?
The Lord is the everlasting God,
the Creator of the ends of the earth.
He will not grow tired or weary,
and his understanding no one can fathom.
He gives strength to the weary
and increases the power of the weak.
Even youths grow tired and weary,
and young men stumble and fall;
but those who hope in the Lord
will renew their strength,
They will soar on wings like eagles;
they will run and not grow weary,
they will walk and not be faint.

—Isaiah 40:28–31

From the High Chair:
Tales of Parenting and Children

CHAPTER 31

Playing House

❦

"Mama, will you play with me?" My preschooler, Emily, always seemed to need my undivided attention when it had already been divided and subdivided. The kitchen clock signaled a half hour until naptime, so I very quickly made a mental list of the chores I needed to accomplish. Patiently, she waited for my delayed reply. Her eyes were hopeful, and I knew that I must put aside my tasks and spend time with her.

"Yes, sweetie. Let's play!" I answered, trying to sound enthusiastic but inwardly wishing I could just finish my housework. She was delighted and skipped off to her playroom. I trailed behind her. My mind was bogged down with the mess I was reluctantly leaving behind. There was a truckload of dirty dishes in the kitchen sink, a laundry basket in the washroom that refused to hold another sock, and a pile of ironing that was quickly beginning to bear a significant resemblance to Mount Everest.

"Come on, Mommy!" she squealed as I reached the playroom strewn with toys. "Let's play house!" For the next thirty minutes, we lived in the world I had long forgotten—the land of make-believe. Honestly, I had not planned to spend any time at play that day. There was so much to be done around the house, and I was short on time. But playing house seemed simple enough to me. After all, we had played house quite often, and I figured I could join in the game with little effort or concentration. As we began our game, a thought occurred to me that I'd never had in past games of playing house.

"Watch her" a small voice seemed to whisper to me. Though I have never heard the audible voice of God, there have been special times in my life when

His words to me were as clear as if He had spoken to me. This was one of these occasions. At the time, I didn't understand His purpose. I was tempted to dismiss the compelling thought, but the small voice persisted. "Watch her closely."

That afternoon, I not only allowed my little daughter to draw me away from the chaos of the household, but I opened my heart to the Lord and invited Him to teach me a very simple yet profound truth that left me rejuvenated and enlightened.

"Here, Mommy. You can dress this one," Emily said. She handed me a doll carefully selected from her collection. We dressed our dolls to her satisfaction. I watched as she took care to be certain their outfits were "just right." Then we hosted them at an elaborate tea party. Emily had planned a complete menu and had set matching dishes in a near perfect order on a small dollhouse table. After the meal was over, it was time for baths. This little mother was careful to provide everything we needed to bathe our dolls effectively: towels, washcloths, and even baby bathtubs made from plastic storage containers for both of us.

"No, Mommy," she said as I began to wash my doll. "You must do it this way!" She took my doll and then proceeded to show me the proper way to bathe the doll. By this time, my interest had heightened. I continued to observe her carefully, eager to see what she would do or say next. *Funny,* I thought to myself. *This game was supposed to be make-believe, but it sure seems a lot like our everyday routine.*

"OK, Mommy. It's time to go to the grocery store," Emily announced as I finished dressing my doll.

"Oh, yes," I replied. I remembered this game, too. Soon we would be filling an old shopping bag with various objects from the playroom store and taking them to the living room corner table—our checkout counter. There, every single item purchased must pass over the imaginary scanner and be redeposited in the shopping bag.

"We do need to visit the store, Emily," I said. The idea of another familiar game appealed to me. To my surprise, though, the game began differently today. It did not start with a collection of items from the playroom store. Nor did it involve an actual trip to the checkout counter in the other room. I was puzzled so I waited for instructions.

"Mommy, first we have to pack the diaper bags," Emily said as she pointed to the two old shopping bags in the corner of the playroom. She pondered over what to include in each bag. When she was confident that she had gathered our most-needed essentials, she carefully loaded hers onto the handlebar of her tricycle—now her car. She handed me the other bag to carry. Without a word, she secured her doll into a car seat that she had made from a crayon canister and also hung it on the handlebars. I was to follow on foot and carry my doll. I continued my observation.

"Mommy, have you seen my keys?" At this I laughed aloud. You could say the lightbulb finally came on or that my elevator reached the top floor. Now I understood why I had been so compelled to watch her play today. This was me. My little girl, though quite unaware of it, had shown me the way she sees me. She was so engrossed in her play that I don't even think she heard my chuckle. Rather, she kept rummaging through her purse until she found the missing keys. We continued to play that afternoon until a cry burst forth from the nursery. My newborn had awakened from her afternoon nap. Carefully, I placed the doll back in her bed, hugged Emily, and left the playroom to check on the baby.

While rocking my newborn, I recounted the events of the afternoon. The mental list of chores made earlier that day was of little significance now. My thoughts were on Emily and the special time we had shared. It seemed only a short time ago that she was the baby in my arms each afternoon. Now she was a small person with budding independence that she displayed more each day. With time passing so quickly, I was reminded that someday, in the not-so-distant future, she too would put down her doll and pick up her own newborn. Oh, how closely she was watching me to learn a mother's love. Now I could see God's purpose for changing my plans on this day. It was to remind me that my mission involves much more than completing a checklist of chores each day, and I was challenged by my little girl...who thought we had only played house.

As Jesus and his disciples were traveling, he came to a village where a woman named Martha opened her home to him. She had a sister called Mary, who sat at the Lord's feet listening to what he said. But Martha was distracted by all the preparations that had to be made. She came to him and asked, "Lord, don't you care that my sister had left me to do the work by myself? Tell her to help me!"

"Martha, Martha," the Lord answered, "you are worried and upset about many things, but only one thing is needed. Mary has chosen the better part, and it will not be taken away from her." (Luke 10:38–42)

(This chapter was originally printed as "Playing House" in *Experiencing God,* May 1994.)

CHAPTER 32

Two Sisters and the Slippery Science Experiment

"WEAR GOGGLES TO PROTECT YOUR eyes," I said as my students blew through plastic straws into large piles of flour, squealing with delight as simulations of moon craters were created. "Don't drink the water from the mudslide made on the sand and water table, and stop daring one another to stick your tongues to the homemade glaciers."

In all my years of teaching science in the elementary classroom, these were just a few recollections of reminders I gave to ensure student safety. Secretly, if I prided myself on anything in my classroom, it was safety. Note to self: never pride myself on anything.

It was a relatively slow evening around our house. No homework, basketball games, or practices, and no Bluebirds or school projects to attend. I jumped at the chance to have an evening to get caught up on work undone around the house. With this rare find of unstructured time, I was around, but I was also a little absentminded that evening.

While I worked, unbeknown to me, my daughters, still in elementary school at the time, decided to do a science experiment in the kitchen. The experiment required only a few materials—a cup of water, a glass, and an oral thermometer. My oldest threw caution to the wind, heating the glass cup of water in the microwave to the boiling point and then immediately sticking the thermometer into the bubbling liquid to measure the temperature. En route to the laundry, I just happened to walk in right after the experiment had been conducted…just in time to witness an eerie quietness in the kitchen. The silence intrigued me, because it rarely happened when these two were together.

"What are you two doing?" I questioned as I stepped into the kitchen. My youngest was wide-eyed, speechless, and waiting to see what her older sister would say or do next. I then noticed steam rising from a glass on the countertop. As I peered into it, my firstborn offered her explanation of their scientific inquiry now gone bad. It seemed that the immediate plunge of the glass thermometer into the boiling liquid had caused the thermometer to break. As she explained this, all I could see now was the ball of mercury floating around near the bottom of the cup. Disposal of this substance was now the question. Carefully, I drained the water from the cup, keeping my eye on the mercury, knowing full well that if it hit any surface it would adhere and cover it like an aggressive amoeba.

What I did next was definitely short of good judgment. Carefully, I tilted the cup, rolling the tiny mercury ball into the palm of my hand, intending to place it in a container and dispose of it properly. Before I could execute my ingenious safety plan, however, the tiny ball rolled downhill and landed right on my wedding ring. I stood there in shock as I watched the substance do exactly what I knew it would do. Within seconds, my shiny gold wedding ring was coated with the mercury. It had now taken on a dull, tarnished silver tint.

The next day, I took the ring to a family friend who was a jeweler. With hopes that he could salvage my ring, I watched as he studied this metallic mess I had made. Puzzled, he shook his head as if to say, *This is a first.* He promised to give it his best shot, and I left less than hopeful. How surprised I was several days later when he called to say that he had been able to restore the ring to its original beauty. As you might imagine, some definite conversation was held that day concerning the conducting of future science experiments. Also, I had to come to grips that I too had not acted very responsibly. After all, who picks up a ball of mercury? Not a rocket science moment for me.

Maybe you feel shiny like my newly refurbished ring, or perhaps you feel a little tarnished from the happenings of life that seem to be clouding your perspective or sapping your spiritual strength. Regardless of where you stand at this moment, be encouraged. God says new beginnings happen, not only once a year, but rather every month, week, day, hour, and even second for us to begin again restored and free in Christ. God's perfect measure of grace and mercy can wash over the ills of our lives, cleansing and making us shining examples once again of His perfect work of redemption in our lives.

The word of God promises:

Because of the Lord's great love we are not consumed,
for his compassions (mercies) never fail.
They are new every morning;
great is your faithfulness.

—Lamentations 3:22–23

Miss Dixie's House

MISS DIXIE'S HOUSE SAT HIGH on a hill at the end of a winding road. It wasn't much to look at unless you were a regular visitor there. It was easy to miss the magic of such a place. The shingles on the old house were weathered and drooping, having sustained many West Texas storms that blew through the town over the years. A heaping mound of dirt sat off in the distance in the large yard where we played many games of King of the Mountain, and an old abandoned car was parked right in the center. It had a mystical, transforming quality for all who entered inside. With the closing of its old creaky doors, we were transported to any place we chose to go. There were old chicken coops—now clean and empty—that made a great place to hold a clubhouse meeting before the sun began to beat down too heavily on the yard. The old screen door on the side of the house made a creaking sound each time it opened. We kept our eyes on the old door, for when it flew open with Miss Dixie standing in the threshold, we knew it was time to eat. No dinner bell needed!

Once inside, the house always smelled of fried potatoes and other comfort foods. Miss Dixie lined the children up around the old dining room table. There was usually some quarreling about whose turn it was to sit on the long wooden bench that rested on one side of the table, while others finished their chattering brought in from the outdoors. When all was quiet, she would say grace, and we would all dig in and eat until we'd had our fill. In the afternoons, the fans were turned on, and the faint smell of oil paints and pastels filtered throughout the rooms as Miss Dixie worked on her portraits, taking the darkness out of black-and-white photographs and adding color that made them come to life. She was the first artist I had ever known.

Most afternoons, with rest time over, we would return to the yard to play until parents began arriving. One particular day, I knew rest time would not be followed by an afternoon of playing outside. It was raining, and on this kind of day, Miss Dixie had board games, cards, or cartoons playing on her old black-and-white TV. It was at times like this that, without my attention diverted to something of my liking, I would miss Mama. Miss Dixie knew this about me. I must have been looking a little drab one day because, without even questioning me, she left her afternoon routines. Without speaking, I watched as she gathered an assortment of supplies, including old cardboard boxes, pencils, scissors, and glue. My curiosity grew as she sat down beside me and began to create for me a lovely cardboard dollhouse. I was amazed. Although I had a beautiful dollhouse at home, I was falling more in love with this interesting creation by the minute. When she had completed the construction, she did not stop but rather began to draw, cut out, and glue together pieces of furniture for the house. This had certainly done the trick! I'd now forgotten completely about all I was missing—both Mama and playing outside. The rain fell, but it didn't matter anymore. For the rest of the afternoon, I was contentedly occupied with the dollhouse.

Though over forty years have passed, I thank God for the gift of this memory. I can still recall that afternoon, the dollhouse, and most importantly, the comforting spirit of Miss Dixie, who spoke from her heart to care for me and the other children entrusted to her each day.

In memory of Dixie Sims, December 11, 1925, to February 9, 2004.

And He took the children in his arms, placed his
hands on them and blessed them.

—Mark 10:16

CHAPTER 34

The No-Pets Policy and a Gazillion Gerbils

FOR TWO PARENTS WHO AGREED prior to having children that we would be a pet-free family, I would have to say we…failed. Recently, while unloading the storage room in order to do ceiling repairs, I opened a dusty old plastic tub that was home to mementos from my years as a first-grade teacher. Rummaging through the container, I found a small metal plaque engraved with the words *Peanut Butter* nestled unassumingly between some papers. As I picked it up, I was reminded that this was the beginning of our life as pet owners.

Maybe we would have been more successful at remaining pet-free if we had given thought to the fact that our children's preschool had a live barnyard, complete with ducks, bunnies, and at one point, baby goats. If this was not enough to get our attention, the science lab on campus should have been. My girls loved the lab. It was a regular petting zoo, complete with a bird, snake, fish, and iguana, and a pair of very social ferrets that on occasion could be seen roaming the halls riding on a remote-control car. While this most likely violated every health code possible, it sparked a love for God's creatures in the hearts of my children. So it should have been no surprise the day our daughter came home with the news that her class had been blessed with a gazillion gerbils and asked could she please, pretty please have some. Not *one*, but *some*. I wanted so desperately to say, "Absolutely not," but after her persuasion, I simply could not say no. We agreed to take two of the squirmy rodents—and only two—on one condition. She must make certain that we had two females or two males.

The days of anticipation were underway as we waited reluctantly and she waited expectantly for the appointed time when we could bring the little creatures home. Just like a new mother, my daughter was busy preparing for their arrival. Soon, the day came. We were now the proud grandparents and our daughter the parent of two male gerbils…or so we thought.

The furry critters were very happy in the condo we purchased for them and ran tirelessly in a little plastic ball all over our house for added exercise. With the exception of a few mishaps—such as leaving the cage open or not securing the tubes that ran outside the house and having to search the house for them—life was fine. This thing called pet ownership really wasn't so bad. That was the belief until one memorable morning. I awoke early and did my usual sleepwalking into the kitchen to feed my caffeine habit when all of a sudden I heard some rustling in the cage. It appeared that one of the gerbils was frantically kicking the wood shavings all over something. A closer look caused one immediate reaction—screaming! Inside the cage were many small, gooey pink creatures that had not been there the night before. It became very clear at that moment that *we did not have two males, nor did we have two females.* So on that day, we took the leap forward an entire generation and became great grandparents, and our eight-year-old daughter was now the grandparent of multiple gerbils!

Feeling a little sick, I went to work that morning frantically thinking about how to get rid of some of the new dwellers. If not, we were about to be the owners of a gerbil farm. I could see where this was going—they would continue to multiply. I frantically weighed the options. The only thing I could do was to follow in the steps of our daughter's teacher. I could do just as she had done. Pulling into the drive at school, I decided that I would ask for families to take one, two, or more of these little darlings, help me spread the love a little, and disband the impending truth that I would soon be a gerbil farmer.

That year I opened the first ever adoption agency for gerbils in my first-grade classroom. The qualifications for pet ownership were very simple: come with a parent permission slip and a suitable cage with food and water. Until adoption day, we took turns tending to the masses. The time finally came when we could share our gerbil fortune with eager students. We kept the mother and one of the babies. Our daughter named him Peanut Butter, and she loved him for as long as he lived.

Much later, we gathered in the backyard for Peanut Butter's memorial service. He had been carefully placed in a checked box that had been decorated by a little girl who was mourning the loss of a much-loved pet. By now, the plan of being a no-pet family was far from our minds. Somehow we had never considered the value of the lessons our children could learn from having pets: the opportunities to put something above themselves, to love unconditionally as pets do, and to experience loss in a small way that prepares us for greater heartbreaks in life as we grow older. Through the years, we have opened our home to a pair of abandoned baby sparrows; stray cats Brown Kitty, Billy Bob, and Boots; and our own shelter-adopted cat, Rosie, who still lives with us today. Our hearts are full, and our memories are sweet. We will never be the same, and it all began with a gazillion gerbils!

Until one has loved an animal, a part of one's soul remains not awakened.

—Anatole France

CHAPTER 35

Beetles in the Bedroom

I TAUGHT SCHOOL IN A nearby town during the week while our two girls were growing up. They each went to different schools on opposite ends of the city. Therefore, it could sometimes be a logistical nightmare for everyone to get up, get organized, and get out the door and arrive at their destination on time. I learned early on to choose my battles when it came to weekday morning routines. While most of my mothering friends had strict guidelines for their children's rooms during the week, I have to admit I did not. If they were able to get through the room and find their belongings and appropriate pieces for school uniforms, and nothing was left to grow algae, mold, or any sort of life form, I was happy. That is, until Saturdays rolled around. On Saturday mornings, Mom morphed into a cleaning machine. Not only was *I* cleaning, but they were expected to concentrate on the deep cleaning and organization of their rooms. "No one leaves the house until the rooms are clean," I must have said a million times. This meant no movies, going to friends' houses, or trips to the mall until the work was done. There were weeks this was not such a big deal and they were free for fun by noon. Other weeks I experienced the weeping and gnashing of teeth in my very own living room. As adults, I am sure they remember this ritual; I am waiting to see if they carry on my motherly tradition.

Time certainly flies, and before we knew it, we were down to just one child at home. The regimen continued, much to her disappointment, and it became more and more difficult to complete. I corrected, I complained, and I ranted about the growing mess and disorganization. When I realized my frustration was nearing the rage zone, I decided to stop the madness. How could such a simple request have such a hard follow-through? Finally, one day I snapped. In my opinion, the mess was quickly leading toward a visit from the health department. I was at a loss. "If you do not clean up your room, you are going to be sharing it with creepy crawlers. This room is a breeding ground!" With that said, I turned around and left the room, knowing that I had not affected her in the least.

Desperate times were calling for desperate measures, so I did what any well-meaning parent concerned about the hygienic safety of her child would do. I acquired her father as an accomplice, and our covert operation—Operation Beetle—was born. Our top-secret, brilliant plan was worth a try. What did we have to lose? Careful not to leak any of our strategies, we waited for the perfect time to launch our master plan. On the day we were to invade the territory, we reviewed our checklist.

1) Child has left the premises—check.
2) Room is still in disarray and potentially an invitation for health officials to order a shutdown on the premises—check.
3) Expectations have been clearly communicated on multiple occasions and disregarded or done with less than acceptable outcome—check.

With all points covered, both needing face masks and gloves, we entered the disaster area and planted the answer to this unmanageable problem: a large, black water beetle that had gone on to happier hunting grounds, right in the center of the messy, unmade bed. We concluded our operation by ruffling the bedcovers to look as disheveled as usual. Knowing the beetle wasn't going anywhere, we turned out the light and waited. When she returned, we could hear the familiar sound of the bedroom door creaking as it opened. In a matter of seconds, there was a scream and confirmation for us that change was surely on the way! For the next two hours, I didn't have to say a word—no ranting, no raving, no history lessons of why the room needed to be cleaned. No, there was silence on the parental end and a frantic frenzy could be heard from the condemned zone. In a matter of time, the room looked better than I had seen it in a long time.

To say the room was never messy again would not be accurate. But now when it reached a messy state that was past the point of no return, it was clearly understood that creepy crawlers would be placed—oh, did I really say that? I meant creepy crawlers would somehow find their way into the room. Hmm… crickets anyone?

> *But all things should be done decently and in order.*

> —*1 Corinthians 14:40 esv*

CHAPTER 36

A Heavenly Awakening

WHILE WE WERE RAISING YOUNG children, my husband developed a recurring problem. Every week, he fell asleep in church. Before you judge him too quickly, it wasn't that he lacked devotion or that he did not care about his spiritual growth. Rather, I decided it had something to do with finally being able to experience stillness.

At that point in our lives, church was about the only place moments of serenity could be found. It was here in the pews that no little girls were making promises to him they could never keep when he tried to catch a few winks before dinner. Oh, the vows of silence, stillness, and solitude they would routinely take just to get to nap beside him. Inevitably, though, it would be only minutes before their wiggles would begin, followed by the flailing of their little arms and legs that always crossed over into his sleeping space. Happy tunes in their heads soon followed, and before they knew it they were bursting forth with song...a kind of serenade, I am sure. Nonetheless, there was no sleeping after the final move, when their little fingers lifted his drooping eyelids just to ask, "Daddy, are you really sleeping?"

Also, this sleep-in-church problem surely had something to do with the room itself. After all, the dimness of the lights in the sanctuary naturally invited slumber, as did the lull of beautiful music played throughout the worship time. This serene environment was completely contrary to the one-man bands at home playing out their own renditions on my pots and pans while I cooked dinner.

Quite possibly, it had to do with the silence in the room—never a commodity at our house unless grandparents rescued us for a few hours or maybe a weekend. Even with all these perfectly acceptable reasons why his slumber seemed to set in while at church, it drove me crazy! After all, I reasoned, I wasn't a stranger to sleep deprivation myself. I suffered from the same nap interruptions, not to mention the adventures the middle of the night often brought. I listened to my share of concertos first pounded out on my pots and pans and later on the family piano as "the song of the week" was played repeatedly, with quite a few resounding yet nonbelonging notes to practice for the next day's lesson. I too was tempted with the possibilities for slumber as the lights dimmed. Still, I was somehow able to stay awake in church.

I needed a solution for my husband's routine slumber in the sanctuary for both our sakes, so I set out to find one. First I tried the "elbow method," but I soon realized it had to be repeated every few minutes to be effective, not to mention the sore ribs that followed. Next, I took the romantic approach. If I held his hand, I could inconspicuously squeeze the daylights out of it each time I saw the first signs of slumber approaching. Again, no luck, as his hand became my human stress ball. I was stumped. This problem had to end, or I might as well stay home. Out of sheer desperation, I had one card left. I decided to appeal to his sweet tooth and cash in on the short-lived but effective benefits of sugar. Seemingly, this was my last resort, so I stocked my purse with rolls of sweet-and-sour candy disks, and like a lion looking for its prey, I pounced and promptly prescribed a piece at the first sign of him drifting off. This technique worked, but only a few times. Although he loved sweets, one can only eat so many of those mouth-peeling sweet-and-sour candies in one setting. The reality was he was now burned out on the candy.

The whole plan was an epic fail. Rib poking, hand squeezing, and now abusing the usage of sugar—I had stooped pretty low, I decided. At a total loss and now growing more irritated by the week, I decided to give up. So what if he fell asleep in church? Enough was enough! I quickly crafted a new plan of complacency. My strategy to defeat the sleep monster that continually set in would be simple—I would just let him fall asleep. That's right, I gave my full permission for him to slumber away.

One particular Wednesday, sitting midcenter about the fourth row from the front, signs of slumber again appeared. Sure enough, not too long into the lesson, the all-too-familiar signs appeared...a little head nodding, followed by a burst of wide eyes trying to wake up, and then the last step: a deep breath and straightening of the body. I remembered my vow. I mentally repeated my vow. As much as I wanted to remain unwavering in my decision not to rescue, I failed. This time he not only began to drift off to sleep, but he also began a slight descent forward toward the pew in front of him. *Oh, no!* I thought to myself. *He's going to hit the pew!* This was not an outcome I had considered, so out of panic, I nudged him to stop the fall. Surely this would stop him from sleeping—but it didn't.

After a couple of these episodes, I had truly—and I mean truly—had enough! Right there in the pew, I renewed my vow to not render aid. This time if he fell asleep, I would just let it happen. And it did. Out of the corner of my eye, I could see him leaning forward. He now not only needed rescue from his inopportune time of sleeping but also from his certain collision with the pew in front of him. This time, though my knuckles were white from gripping the pew tightly, I knew I had to refrain. Seconds seemed like hours as his head steadily moved toward the pew in front of us. I braced myself for the fall first with both eyes tightly shut. Then, with just a peek, I saw him suddenly wake up and catch himself by throwing both hands up in the air and raising his feet off the floor as if to say "Glory Hallelujah!" It was as if God had stepped in and woken him up Himself. Unfortunately, the sermon at this point had not warranted any sort of affirmation from the congregation, so this was a moment of awkwardness at its finest. I didn't dare to look around me. The reaction of others would have spoiled the moment, because suddenly I was no longer irritated. Strangely, I was amused.

The battle we had been fighting for months suddenly seemed unimportant and, better yet, resolved. I glanced over at him, only to find him looking at me. We both contained our laughter so as not to disrupt the people around us. Tears were rolling down my cheeks as we silently gave way to laughing until our sides hurt and we were sure we couldn't contain it any longer. The dilemma was solved in a way I could never have imagined. No need for sore ribs, squeezed hands, or overdoses of sugar. With my interventions out of the way and a heavenly awakening, the sleep problem was solved.

I am the LORD, the God of all mankind. Is anything too hard for me?

—*JEREMIAH 32:27*

CHAPTER 37

Parenting Through the Perfect and Prodigal Moments

~~~ ❧ ❧ ~~~

I used to have no children and many theories on raising
them. Now I have many children and no theories.

—JOHN WILMOT

I WAS THE FIRSTBORN IN my family but not the first to give birth. My younger sister became a mother first, and on a number of occasions, I would teasingly say to her, "My children will never do that!" I was half joking but very uninformed at the time about the challenges of parenting. There was a secret pride in my playful comment, which was at least somewhat tongue in cheek. However, many times over, throughout the years of preschool, elementary, middle, and high school, the words I spoke half in jest and half believing had their own way of showing up to haunt me in those times when my two precious gifts were at their finest.

There I was, standing at the counter of a local pizza chain waiting to return a fork and an ample supply of vending machine toys to the cashier. Though I was filled with dread, I was waiting to explain how my five-year-old had managed to use her fork to get exactly what she wanted from the machine. Managing to stick her fork up through the toy exit, she'd discovered that she could hit the mother lode. Really, a five-year-old? I certainly hoped my sister wouldn't hear of this. I knew that her first inclination would be to remind me of my snooty and slightly judgmental words of a few years before. At this moment, I was busted. Feeling a bit repentant for my arrogance and remorsefully eating my sassy words, I waited with confiscated toys in tow, dreading my turn to approach the counter.

With that incident behind us, I was sure nothing of this nature would ever happen again—and yet it did. Soon I found myself face-to-face with a somewhat disgruntled mother trying to kindly tell me her daughter was being denied entrance into the colorful ball pit at the fast food restaurant we often frequented for playdates with friends. Apparently, my oldest had appointed my youngest to stand guard at the entrance and refuse entry to anyone wishing to enter. That's right. No trespassing! My three-year-old took her orders very seriously and refused to let anyone enter the ball house. So there I was again. Teachable moment number two was upon me.

My desperate plan of action consisted of removing the three-year-old, apologizing to the annoyed parent, and deprogramming the idea of an American-style monarchy in the mind of my five-year-old, who was currently hiding in the ball pit. Otherwise, I sensed we would be asked to leave the premises immediately.

Time passed, and there were more prodigal moments in the years to come, along with a few perfect ones. I took my sister's place, and people watched me. I laughed as I recognized their unspoken thoughts: *My child will never do that.* I took no offense, for I knew in that due time *they* would understand that parenting is unpredictable and hard. Soon enough they would experience the snafus of this sacred office. No need to spoil it for them. No need to enlighten them either; their children would take care of that.

Mother of the Year will not be a part of my accolades, but that is not important. I have cherished the good and bad times in the of raising of my children. Through it all, I have come face-to-face with my many weaknesses. I have experienced love and forgiveness, and have been made strong through the privilege of parenting. I have learned immensely from this journey.

My Personal Parenting 101

* Parenting takes time, eating a lot of "humble pie," and sometimes caring more about what your children need to get on the right path than what others may think of you.

- Parenting commands us to bare our souls before the Lord, remove all pretenses, and admit that we do not have all the answers.
- Parenting requires acknowledging that we need help to parent and that the true, single need of our children is to be parented.
- Parenting involves interceding on their behalf, just as Jesus intercedes on our behalf to the Father.
- Parenting involves the seeking of God's will, not our will, for their lives.
- Parenting is not equal to patrolling—we must accept that in spite of our efforts, our children may resist God's path and miss turns designed for their good before yielding.
- Parenting takes patience.
- Parenting calls us to be the constant in their lives.
- Parenting effectively is to practice God's presence and trust His guidance through promises in His word.

The promise of our God is this:
"Train a child in the way he should go,
And when he is old he will not turn from it."

—Proverbs 22:6

From Littles to Middles: Tales from the Schoolroom

CHAPTER 38

The Green Eggs and Ham Brigade

❧

*Teamwork is the ability to work as a group toward a common
vision, even if that vision becomes extremely blurry.*

—*Author Unknown*

FAMILIES WERE ALREADY LINED UP for the most famous school dinner of the year—
green eggs and ham! This was a perfect ending to an already full week of cel-
ebration in honor of the doctor himself. Walking the halls and checking out
the activities going on in each classroom, I made my way to the café where the
highly anticipated dinner was to be served. I was pleased with the turnout as
families lined up to get their share. Before leaving to make my rounds, I decided
to check in with the café staff. The café supervisor looked at me and said six
simple but profound words: *"We are almost out of food."*

These were not the words I had expected to hear, and suddenly I felt a wave
of panic come over me. *What are we going to do? They just keep coming!* My mind
was racing. I had to think fast. About that time, I ran into our counselor, and
we set to work devising a plan to save literally hundreds of kids from being sent
home without green eggs and ham. In a matter of seconds, we were in the car
headed to the grocery store to replenish our lagging supply. Entering the store,
we must have been a blur. I went one way and she went the other to literally
grab as many containers of eggs as we thought we would need. We must have
looked like we were heading home for a feeding frenzy as we checked out. As

we gathered up an absurd amount of egg cartons and yelled back and forth across the store looking for the ham, more fruit punch, and extra green food coloring, no one dared to step in our path! We quickly paid and headed back to school.

The next order of business was to hand off the eggs to the café supervisor...or so we thought. Soon it was discovered that they had no frying pans to scramble the eggs in since the food service company had brought eggs that were already in bags meant to be cooked in hot water.

Now I thought, *What are we going to do with all these eggs?*

Given the growing crowd and the lack of food, it seemed we were working in slow motion, repeatedly tackling obstacles. Never had I imagined that cooking eggs would be such an impossible job!

This was our time. If it was going to happen, it was up to us. With the kitchen ill-equipped for serious egg cooking, we resorted to the next best option: the microwaves in the teachers' lounge. By this time, our head custodian had entered the kitchen and decided to help us get those eggs cooked. We devised a bucket brigade of sorts, and for the next hour the three of us took shifts cooking the green eggs in big plastic bowls and handing them off to a runner who delivered them through the back kitchen door right into the serving line dishes.

That night we made more pans of green eggs and ham than I care to think about! Covered in green splatter, smelling of eggs, and ready to drop from sheer exhaustion, we laughed about the events of the night. Three very different people with very different jobs had come together to devise a plan, solve a problem, and accomplish the work set before us. We were the best scrambled egg team anywhere!

Long ago, men from different walks of life and independent of one another unexpectedly stumbled upon a truth that was so compelling that they had no choice but to leave all and follow after it. Some were fishermen, others were business owners, one was a tax collector, and there was even a revolutionist in the bunch. Maybe they were seeking a change in purpose for their lives, maybe not, but that didn't matter anymore. Jesus had called them. This was their time—individually and collectively. The world had a big problem, and they were called to bring about resolve. Listening to Him, learning from His teachings, and walking in His ways, they became His disciples, His team, so that one day at just the right time they would be ready to share this truth, the Gospel, first with the Jews and then with the Gentiles.

It would be nice if it was as simple as being called and following with no looking back, no denials, no betrayals, and no doubts, but that was just not the case for most of those followers then…or for us now. As willing as they were to serve, they had detours, failures, and all-out disbelief at times. However, Jesus did not give up on this eclectic group. By the same token, He also does not give up on us. As His children, we know the world has a problem—it desperately needs the truth of the Gospel. As believers, we are God's team to carry out the heart of His mission: salvation for every man, woman, and child on the earth.

Help us to be compelled to share your message, for the time is short.
Help us to be kind and compassionate that we may draw others to you.
Help us to forgive and not take offense quickly and unnecessarily.
Help us to be trustworthy.
May our prayer be that everyone we come in contact with will see the difference
in our lives because we know you personally and surrender to you.
Amen

For God so loved the world that he gave his one and only Son, that
whoever believes in him shall not perish but have eternal life.

—John 3:16

CHAPTER 39

The Task, the Teacher, and the Tidy Bowl Man

IT WAS SUMMER BREAK, AND I was busy at the school, acting as the receptionist for the annual summer academy. I enjoyed this break from routine, as I was assigned more carefree tasks and got to see students outside the structured classroom setting. On this particular morning, the hall was desolate and no one was available to give me a much-needed break, so I decided to just carry the phone with me in case someone needed to get a message through.

All was well until I made the fatal mistake of deciding to stop by the ladies' room on the way back. Within seconds, when I was already in a stall, it happened: "Ring…ring, ring…" Immediately, I panicked. My mind was frantically trying to rationalize the best option. *What do I do? Now? Here? Really?*

What seemed like minutes was really only a matter of seconds. I decided to go for it and answer the call. After all, I reasoned, the person on the other end of the line would have no idea where I was, so no one would be the wiser. I listened intently, taking down the message mentally. I was almost ready to hang up, having managed to get through this awkward situation, until…I had forgotten one little detail. As soon as I stood up, the Tidy Bowl man came out with a vengeance! Again I was paralyzed. I was mortified. Was the swooshing sound really this loud any other time? It now appeared I had yet another drastic decision to make in three of the longest minutes I had ever experienced.

Should I explain? I asked myself. *No, I don't even know this person,* I reasoned. *Should I apologize for the noise and make something up?* Again, I decided that would make it more obvious that I was covering up. So I did what I thought was best—nothing.

With all the composure I could muster. I stood firm in my tracks so as not to awaken my foe from the bowl again, completed the call, and promptly delivered the message. I still laugh every time I think about this mishap. Isn't it amazing how even with something as comical as this situation, God still comes through?

To me, it is a reminder, much like the one Jesus gave to His disciples as He sent out the twelve. They would be entering conditions that would be less than desirable. The situations they would encounter would be challenging and at times full of uncertainty. Jesus encouraged them to face the issues at hand with confidence that God himself would not only see them through but would give them the words to say for the moment through the Holy Spirit. He charged them to do one thing—stand firm.

At that time you will be given what to say, for it will not be you speaking, but the Spirit of your Father speaking through you.

—Matthew 10:19–20

There is nothing concealed that will not be disclosed, or hidden that will not be made known.

—Matthew 10:26

CHAPTER 40

The Ice Cream Lineup

A FIRST-GRADE CLASSROOM IS QUITE an interesting organism. While some characteristics of this entity no doubt are the same child to child—such as the opinion that recess is actually a mandated subject, that no one should eat the green peas on their tray, and that their teacher (me) really lives at the school—there are things that remind me of the importance of looking at them as individual children, each possessing traits that are unique to him or her. Whenever I was able to grab that quick moment of stillness, I noticed that the classroom was much like a body—sometimes a disjointed body, but nevertheless a body.

It didn't take long to locate the student who was holding the room together. He or she would be moving about, quietly checking to see that everyone else was doing what they were supposed to be doing. Another student would be taking notes about the injustices occurring and would be quick to tell me about the unfairness of it all or debrief me on wrongful acts that may have occurred behind my back or right under my nose. There would be another student who would be greatly disturbed by the "progress" all over the floor and would quickly move about, cleaning up paper scraps and arranging books on the shelves. Just standing back, though it could be annoying at times—especially when I had been tattled to for the billionth time—I had to admit, we all had our place...even Marvin.

Marvin never seemed interested in supervising the classroom or reporting the various crimes that occurred on a daily basis. Nor was he ever bothered by the mess—or "progress"—that accumulated on the floor. Disarray within the classroom was no problem for him. No, Marvin cared about one thing—perfecting his craft of persuasion. I would rarely hear anything from Marvin. Until

I had to question something, he was pretty much seen but not heard. Then, for some reason, his name would most always surface in the following context: "But Marvin said…" Not that the suggestions he was making to the students were harmful or bad, but rather they were from his perspective, the way he saw things, and this never rang truer than on ice cream day.

In our small school, we did not have a cafeteria. Daily, students would file by the tiny kitchen window at the end of the hall and take a tray back to the classroom to eat lunch. The students would set out paper placemats they had made, and for thirty minutes a day, we would turn our classroom into a lunch-room. As a class, we agreed to rules so that our lunch etiquette would make dining pleasant for all, including the expectations for ice cream day, the most coveted day of the week. The main rule was that no one was to leave his or her seat with ice cream in his or her hands.

On one ice cream day, I stepped just outside the door for a minute while the students were enjoying their ice cream to answer a colleague's question. When I turned around in the doorway, I found only empty chairs. The entire class was lined up in a straight line, quiet, facing forward, and—yes—licking their ice cream bars. I immediately asked, "What are you doing? You know we stay seated with ice cream!" One child stepped forward and simply said, "Marvin said we would have our ice cream outside today." At that, I knew I had a choice to make. Was the reprimand really worth it? The chairs and tables were tidy and the students were standing in perfect order quietly, and it just seemed wrong to undo all that.

While I was certain that Marvin had masterminded the plan, in that short period of time he really only had time to state the plan. From that point, the overseer of the room must have helped to get everyone organized, with the classroom helper reminding them to clean up, push in their chairs, and get in a neat, orderly line. The one who always sung of injustice rehearsed his speech should I not grant the wish. Soon he would be telling me that after all they had done it was just unfair if we didn't get to go outside. What was I to do? So I smiled, admired their teamwork, admitted it did seem like a good idea, and led them to the playground to enjoy a few minutes of sunshine, dripping ice cream, and sticky fingers.

My students from that class are now grown. They have careers, and some have families of their own. I am sure the uniqueness they displayed as first graders has in some way shaped who they are in adulthood. My prayer is that they have put their passions to good use to serve others in a manner that honors the Savior we spent time learning about that first-grade year. The differences seen in those children paint a vibrant picture of what God says about the Body of Christ.

Isn't it great to not be just like everyone else? To have our own strengths, weaknesses, talents, and interests?

> *But in fact God has placed the parts in the body, every one of them,*
> *just as he wanted them to be. If they were all one part, where would*
> *the body be? As it is, there are many parts, but one body.*

> —1 CORINTHIANS 12:18–20

Ten Things That Show You're an Elementary School Teacher

1. You sing "Baby Beluga" all the way home from work.
2. Your students talk to you through the grates in the door of your classroom restroom.
3. You spread butter on your bread at lunchtime with a craft stick.
4. You spend time every day reminding students that boogies are not a food group.
5. You wear every gift given to you during the class Christmas party at the same time.
6. You own no clothes that do not have at least one marker or paint stain.
7. You think speaking in rhyme is a normal pattern of speech.
8. You are bilingual: English and children's.
9. You spend hours in the grocery store aisles each year figuring out how prepackaged food containers might be reused in your classroom *and* you throw nothing away.
10. You tell your own family to line up when it is time to leave for church.

My earliest recollection of considering teaching as a profession was playing school with my sisters. We would take my mother's old quilts and drape them over the dining room chairs to create a classroom. Within these cloth walls, I would spend hours instructing my sisters, dolls, or anything that would listen. Much later, long after the days of playing school had passed, I began to think about the overwhelming question of "What am I going to do with the rest of my life?"

I clearly remember one afternoon before graduation when I went out to my dad's garage and said, "Daddy, what do you think I should do when I graduate?"

He didn't hesitate but quickly replied, "I think you should be a teacher."

He went on to give me all the reasons why it would be the best profession for me. I vaguely remember some of his reasons, but I vividly remember the confirmation in my heart that teaching would be the right path for me. Once I set out on that path, I never looked back. I wish I had written down more of the experiences I've had, but I hold most of them in my heart. For me, it was and still is not just a job. It is among the highest of callings.

Father,

May I be renewed today and remember my purpose in this profession that you have blessed me with. Help me be slow to speak, quick to listen, and kind to a fault. Remind me to place them before myself and consider their good above my own. Help me to correct with care and dignity those needing redirection. May I look at the children I encounter every day and see them for what they really are—precious gifts sent by parents, grandparents, and guardians who are counting on me to give them my best because they have sent to me their very best. Most of all, may I point them to you.

Amen

> *Jesus said, "Let the little children come to me, and do not hinder them, for the kingdom of heaven belongs to such as these."*
>
> *—Matthew 19:14*

CHAPTER 42

What's in a Name?

IT'S INTERESTING TO DISCOVER HOW people receive their names. Sometimes parents are intent on carrying on the family name, while others are more focused on the meaning of a name. Still others toss it up to just sheer liking when choosing. However names are arrived at, they're important identification tags we wear as the process of defining who we really are begins.

"Hi, Mrs. Bell!" I quickly turned to see a teenage girl approaching me with her parents following behind. Suddenly, a wave of panic rushed over me. I could feel my face getting flushed. I tried to control the rapid eye movement and nervousness that was becoming more apparent by the second. Although I recognized her as a former student, I couldn't remember her name. I had to think fast!

Should I pretend to know her and take a chance on the name? After all, I had it narrowed it down to two. *Or should I just confess and ask for forgiveness, stating the truth that my memory had failed me again as it often did after so many years of classrooms?*

I decided to take the chance and call her by name. "Hello, Kristen," I replied. Immediately, I saw a look of puzzlement on her face. As her parents looked on, she explained that she was not that person. I was mortified for both of us and could have kicked myself for foolishly taking the chance. Immediately, I reverted to my second option and apologized, blamed my memory, and tried to divert the awkwardness of the situation by talking about what she was now doing. I am sure her parents were less than impressed with my excuse. Even though I had only had her in class for one period of one semester, this girl was her parents' world, and I loathed myself for not remembering her name.

As I was trying to comfort myself concerning this embarrassing experience, I realized that while her name had escaped me, I vividly remembered a lot of other things about her. I could remember the year I taught her and where she sat in the classroom—right side of the back row, aisle seat. I recalled her classroom personality—helpful and quiet but confident—and that she was an excellent student. So what was most important to remember: her given name or all the things to which her name was linked? Her personal qualities had certainly made a lasting impression in my memory.

For the sake of the student's feelings, I would venture to say *both* are important, but the scripture seems to speak more to what is linked to a person's name and the importance of this rather than giving attention simply to the name itself. The word of God refers to this as a "good name." Below are three thoughts that align with God's word concerning the importance of a good name before humankind and God.

* A good name is valuable.

> *A good name is more desirable than great riches; to be*
> *esteemed is better than silver or gold. (Proverbs 22:1)*

* A good name is part of a God-pleasing testimony.

> *Let love and faithfulness never leave you; bind them*
> *around your neck, write them on the tablet of your heart.*
> *Then you will win favor and a good name in the sight of*
> *God and man. (Proverbs 3:4)*

* A good name is lasting.

> *A good name is better than fine perfume, and the day of*
> *death better than the day of birth. (Ecclesiastes 7:1)*

I know what you're thinking. Maybe this seems impossible. I too have had that same thought at times. *I might as well give up on having a good name before men and*

God. *I have a zillion past mistakes, wrong attitudes, and some pretty big failures! What's worse is that others know about some of them. People surely won't forget my shortcomings, and that disqualifies me from having a "good name" before others as well as before the Lord.*

Not so! The Bible says God knows our names. He sees His children differently than we see ourselves. As believers in Him, ones who are forgiven and fully trusting, He sees us not for what we once were but for what we have become through Him.

> *He calls his own sheep by name.*
>
> —John 10:3

Lord,
Help me in spite of my past shortcomings and failures to have a good name that can be a testimony—valuable, God-pleasing, and lasting.
Amen

CHAPTER 43

Lights, Camera, Action!

DURING MY SEVENTEEN YEARS OF being a classroom teacher, my favorite subject to teach was math. For me, it was the subject that brimmed with possibilities for fun as well as learning. Sometimes we counted patterns of numbers or memorized math facts or algorithms to catchy tunes. Other times we played games of intrigue, such as Math Battleship to learn coordinates. We had competitions that credited someone in the classroom as the mathematician of the day. Often, gold stars would be seen on the desks of students who had worked cooperatively and demonstrated levels of higher-order thinking. We called this kind of thinking "Gold Star Thinking," and the students coveted possessing the shiny gold stars for the class period.

One particular day in early spring, the door to my classroom was flung open. Five visitors filed in with clipboards in hand and large paper cutout cameras hung from their necks. Lights, cameras, action! It was a district walk-through. I felt a twitch of concern rise up within me. Today, of all days, we were not doing anything spectacular. *If only they had come yesterday,* I thought.

The day before, we had held the Linear Math Olympics in our classroom. The students long-jumped over an imaginary pit, threw a paper-plate discus, and had a linear relay with cotton balls and straws, just to name a few. But today…well, I deemed it pretty ordinary.

The observing group moved about the room gathering information and writing down their observations. The students continued their activity of measuring objects from a paper bag as if company had not come to visit. I was the only one ill at ease.

Secretly, I had always prided myself on being able to stay calm, collected, and focused during walkthroughs. Today, my pride got the best of me. This surprise visit, I must admit, had me slightly intimidated. I was concentrating very hard on keeping my poker face on so as to hide the worrisome thoughts that swirled through my head. *Maybe this isn't what they wanted to see. Should I explain?* I thought.

Though our guests only stayed a few minutes, it seemed like an eternity. As the five continued to watch the children, the inevitable happened. My thoughts were suddenly redirected to a heated argument in the back of the room. I immediately went to the students to resolve the issue, hoping it could be handled quickly. Again a negative thought returned. *A classroom fight is all I need—what will they think?*

By the time we had resolved the issue, the visitors had vanished as quickly as they had arrived. Later that day, I asked my principal about the afternoon observation. The heated argument while our guests were present had me slightly miffed. There was a long pause and little emotion in her voice as she replied. "Well, I guess they needed time to work it out."

This was not at all what I expected to hear, but it was all I needed to hear. She hadn't seen the same mundane lesson that I convinced myself I had taught that day. She hadn't thought twice about the skirmish between the boys. What she saw was a successful day in my classroom as children worked together, learned from one another, and successfully worked through conflict and accomplished the task set before them.

The lesson I prepared for the children had turned into a lesson for me.

I am grateful for that day. It took me from my comfort zone to a deeper understanding of what God holds as important in my classroom. It forever changed my way of thinking. Wanting the approval of others is a natural thing, but it is not a Godly thing when it consumes me, causes me to measure my worth in any area of my life by it, and/or takes my eyes off my students' needs. I guess *I* just needed time to figure that out!

Am I now trying to win the approval of human beings, or of
God? Or am I trying to please people? If I were still trying
to please people, I would not be a servant of Christ.

—Galatians 1:10

123

CHAPTER 44

The Great Giving Mix-Up

As MAGICAL A TIME AS Christmas always is in an elementary classroom, one thing that I never could quite see the enchantment in was the gift exchanges at Christmas parties. I tried them all—book exchanges, name exchanges, luck-of-the-draw exchanges, and silly games to accomplish all of the above. I discovered that all methods had certain similarities, and no matter how great or how poor the gift was deemed, it was always a toss-up as to what would follow. While some students would be elated with the gift they received, others would not.

No matter how well I tried to prepare them to be grateful for the present they received, it never failed that at this young age students would show their feelings about what they received in a variety of ways. Those who were thrilled with what was inside their packages would be instantly showing others and totally caught up in the gift. If the item received was a bit less favored or possibly wholeheartedly disliked, some would just silently put it away, while others would begin the bargaining process to try and make a trade they felt would be more to their liking. Usually a few would be lamenting or in some cases howling to everyone within earshot to show their disappointment. Regardless of how the disenchanted students reacted, the result was the same—disappointment for both the giver and the receiver.

After several years of repeating this torturing tradition because it was what all the other classrooms were doing, I decided Room 304 had to make a change. So the following year, I announced to my students that the Christmas party would be a little different this year in that we would not be receiving gifts but giving gifts instead. The students looked puzzled. How could you have one without the other? As I explained that our local shelter had a great need for winter outerwear such as hats, scarves, and mittens, as well as toiletries, the attention of the students seemed to be more drawn in to what I was saying. As we talked, I learned that some did not know what a shelter was or that sometimes even children had to go and live there. I continued to share the plan with them, informing them that we would be taking up a collection of these items and placing them under our tree until the day of the party. On that day, we would box them up and send them to the shelter so that families would have them before Christmas. We even extended our idea to the other classrooms in our hallway, and many joined us in carrying out the project.

Even though the students had been eager to participate, on the day of the party I was a little apprehensive about the mood in the room when children realized we *really* were not exchanging gifts. However, my worries were relieved and I knew that this was the right decision for our room when the students saw that we had outgrown the small place under our tree for collecting the items. Boxes were overflowing with the gifts from the students in our classroom and hallway. I think that year my intention to teach my students a thing or two about gratefulness and giving was accomplished not only in their hearts but in mine as well. That year, both young and old alike were either reminded or came to the understanding for the very first time that the joy of gifts is really never about the getting but rather the giving.

So what about the other 364 days of the year? What could giving look like the rest of the year? The book of John in the New Testament of the Bible tells the parable of the widow and the coins. Jesus tells us she traveled to the temple to present her offering of two coins that didn't even add up to a single penny in value. These two coins were not only her offering, but they were all she had to live on. I am sure that some people who witnessed her giving her offering that day were wondering why she even bothered. Others may have judged her as irresponsible and unwise and even a little out of touch with the reality of her situation. Didn't she realize that she had no retirement pension or government assistance coming her way? Had she thought about the fact that she was too old to get a job? The parable ends with Jesus declaring her offering worth far more than any other received that day. How could this be? This woman's giving was not a fraction of the wealth still waiting for her in a bank account somewhere. No, her giving was sacrificial. It was truly all that she had, and it cost her everything.

What about us? Does that mean we should all go empty our bank accounts? Not necessarily, but as we walk through this year, there are blessings awaiting us through opportunities to give of our money, time, or talents that we can easily miss without a sacrificial heart. When giving costs us something, when there is nothing in it for us personally, there is a joy that will overcome us that is unmatched and beyond explanation. In giving we are really getting!

Calling His disciples to him, Jesus said:

> *"Truly I tell you, this poor widow has put more into the treasury*
> *than all the others. They all gave out of their wealth; but she, out*
> *of her poverty, put in everything—all she had to live on."*

—Mark 12:43–44

CHAPTER 45

Forgotten Prayer

THERE THEY WERE, ALL SIXTEEN of them. It was their first day of fourth grade and my first day in the school. Millions of thoughts swirled through my head. *God, what am I doing here? Are you sure this is the right address?* There were no familiar faces giving me any indication that I was one of them yet. I waited, thinking of the times in years past when kids would come into the room and say, "Oh! I hoped I would be in your room!" This time, no one said a word. Mechanically I moved throughout the day. I hated to admit it, but I wasn't sure I could love these children like I had loved the students, siblings, and parents of my former campus. What was I to do? Realizing I had to get rid of these negative feelings, I simply said, "Lord, I ask you to help me love these children."

The months passed, and things got easier. Giggles began to creep in. I was included in the "what happened over the weekend" stories, and once again I had handmade pictures and interesting gifts that made their way out of pockets and lunchboxes. I was not even aware that I was no longer consciously praying the words I had uttered out of desperation on that first day of school. In fact, I had all but forgotten them until the last week...

She had come into the room on that first day with a presumption that she would probably not like me and that I most likely would not like her. Therefore, there would be no reason for me to believe I could do anything to help her. She didn't offer a square inch of effort to get to know me for much of the year. Every response, reaction, or ounce of participation that I could muster from her took great effort.

It was during the last week of school that she arrived with a handmade gift. I was surprised, not only by the gesture, but by what I read:

B—Best teacher
E—Every time makes me laugh
L—Laughs a lot
L—Loves children

I was doing well reading the poster until I reached the last line. The words jumped off the page, and suddenly I remembered my desperate cry months earlier. My prayer had been answered, and today was confirmation day! Of all students, she felt loved. My few prayerful words uttered on that first day were sincere, but oh how I underestimated how seriously God was taking the situation. He knew her need as well as the needs of the other fifteen students he purposefully placed in my classroom. Such a vivid reminder of God's faithfulness to answer prayer! That was years ago, but I will never forget the effect it had on my life. Even those simple and sometimes desperate prayers are still important to God.

For the eyes of the Lord are on the righteous and
his ears are attentive to their prayer.

—*1 Peter 3:12*

The Dime Disaster

It was midafternoon, and my first-grade class was buzzing with busyness. The children were scattered throughout the room working on assigned centers with their peers. As usual, I was circling the room checking to see that all was well. I turned to see one of my students standing right beside me.

"Mrs. Bell, Mrs. Bell, Teddy has a dime up his nose!"

Struggling to process exactly what he had said, I replied, "A what?"

He repeated, "A dime. Teddy has a dime up his nose!"

I quickly located Teddy in the classroom to assess the accuracy of this message for myself. It was true. Teddy did have a dime in his nose. It was so far up in there that I could barely see the silver rim of the coin.

While Teddy was calm and seemed undisturbed by the whole thing, the sense of well-being I had felt only seconds before had vanished. I immediately went into interrogation mode, anxious to find out how this happened, who did it, and what on earth for!

"Teddy, how did this happen?" I asked him, trying to remain calm. After all, this was not your typical center-time disturbance.

Teddy replied, "Jake said I couldn't do it. He dared me to prove it."

At this point, Jake was speechless. He and I knew he was busted, but for now, the urgency was with Teddy. My mind was racing, my heart rate was climbing past a safe aerobic level, and I wasn't sure what to do. So I did what any experienced teacher would do without the presence of a nurse on campus. I took Teddy straight to the principal's office. I had the utmost confidence in our principal and hoped that she would not fail me now. After assessing the situation, she pulled out a long pair of tweezers and pulled the dime right out of his nose! Teddy was relieved and I was relieved, but I was still wondering how he ever got it up there in the first place.

This story provides us with a twist of irony. If we are not careful, we will be walking around with the same proverbial dime shoved right up our own noses—all in the name of acceptance. Whether consciously or subconsciously like Teddy, we also face a challenger. The scripture refers to him as the *father of lies* (John 8:44). He works endlessly to convince us that the acceptance we are longing for can be found in people, possessions, careers, and a vast array of other things. He uses our personal weaknesses to wear us out trying to gain it! We would be wise to remember what God's word has to say about true acceptance that is only found in Him.

Long before he laid down earth's foundations, he had us in mind, had settled on us as the focus of His love, to be made whole and holy by his love. Long, long ago he decided to adopt us into His family through Jesus Christ.

—*Ephesians 1:3–6 msg*

Very truly I tell you, whoever accepts anyone I send accepts me; and whoever accepts me accepts the one who sent me.

—*John 13:20*

Accept one another, then, just as Christ accepted you, in order to bring praise to God.

—*Romans 15:7*

CHAPTER 47

God's Jobs

TIDYING UP THE COUNTERTOPS IN my classroom, I picked up a stack of journals that had been returned hastily and without regard for neatness or order. As I began to straighten the stack, the thought occurred to me, "Better take a look at these." In my mind, there was a hint of doubt that my students had fully completed their assignments. Although I wasn't normally so skeptical, it was the week before Christmas break, and this time in the academic year is not known as the most productive. As I looked at them, my eyes skimming the pages for the verse I had assigned, the illustrations I had required, and the students' written responses demonstrating their understanding of the verse, I quickly made mental notes of those who had taken their assignment seriously and those who would need a little encouragement to get finished. However, when I reached the bottom of the stack, the writings in one journal caused me to do more than just glance inside.

This journal was different. For this day's writing, there was no elaborate illustration but only a simple golden crown drawn in the middle of the page. As I read the verse I had given that day and considered her response, suddenly the messiness of the books and a million other end-of-the-day tasks seemed unimportant. Neatly, completely, and in her best handwriting, the student wrote:

For to us a child is born,
to us a son is given,
and the government will be on his shoulders.
And he will be called

Wonderful Counselor, Mighty God,
Everlasting Father, Prince of Peace. (Isaiah 9:6)

Though I had read or heard this verse so many times before, I would have missed the message if I had stopped short of reading her response:

This means to me that Jesus has many names and
jobs that He willingly does for us.

—Kathy

It was simple, yet profound. Biblical scholars, authors, and commentators have written journals, given lectures and sermons, and published volumes of works expounding on this verse, but today there was such beauty in simplicity. Jesus took His assignment from God the Father very seriously; He completed it with perfection in order to make us complete. It was a messy job full of conflict from an unruly people—some in disbelief and others who could not understand or appreciate the exchanges He made. Royalty for lowliness? A Kingly crown for a crown of thorns? Not surprised by this puzzlement, He stayed the course and finished the mission through the virgin birth, sinless life, death, and resurrection for our salvation.

Somehow, He looks past our offenses of forgetting His wonder and takes the opportunity, such as this one today, to remind us of just that. We are always on His mind. Day in and day out, He provides us wise counsel through His word if we will but stop, be still, be silent, and listen. When we least expect it and need it most, He affirms that He is our Everlasting Father, our Prince of Peace for all times.

In that one sentence, the truth became alive for me again. There was nothing more to say. I closed her journal and knew I would never look at all Christ was called to do on my behalf in the same way I had before. That day, I completed my own jobs with a little more spring in my step.

CHAPTER 48

The Principal's Principle

*You must give up the life you planned in order to
have the life that is waiting for you.*

—JOSEPH CAMPBELL

I AM AMAZED WHEN I see athletes performing the sport of cliff diving. Gracefully and skillfully, toned, poised people dive into the dark, deep waters that are calmly moving and rolling many feet beneath them. While I am curious to catch a glimpse of their facial expressions right before this feat, their body language seems to say, "I've got this."

Such was not the case four years ago when I was assigned my first assistant principal job at a neighboring elementary school in our district. Though I had been an educator for seventeen years, the waters that first year rolling and billowing beneath my feet were anything but serene. Rather, they were rough and uncharted, and they required frequent navigational changes and exuberant strength when the floodgates opened without warning. Looking back, I have to admit that at the beginning of this journey, I had nothing! How could I be in a field for so long and have nothing? Quickly, I learned to chart the course, navigate through calm waters, and ride the storms, even though I never knew from which direction the blessings or calamities would come. This leap (not a swan dive) delivered quite an adventure.

I have always been a goal setter. This has been true of me in both my personal and professional life, so I planned, worked hard, and did everything I could do to achieve my goals. Sometimes I succeeded, and sometimes I did not. This particular assignment—one that was not an original part of my plan—caught me off guard. Nevertheless, I dove in, still a little saddened that things had not completely gone as planned yet grateful to have the opportunity to use the training I had worked so hard to complete.

Over time my desires began to change. The direction of my heart was repositioned, and God whittled away more of the old controlling and, yes, somewhat manipulating me. The change in attitude wasn't a sudden shift, an immediate heart change, or anything drastic I can point to that happened at a specific time. Instead, the changing of my heart was much like a tide rolling in to quench the surface of a thirsty beach and then receding back into the waters, carrying with it things no longer needed along the shoreline.

Today is the last day I will ever spend with the staff of my school. It is bittersweet, but it is right. We've gone a lot of miles together. We've shared one another's hurts and happiness, been disappointed and delighted, and most importantly, have worked together to make things better for our students. We have grown as professionals.

Once again, I am back at the top of the same cliff. All too familiar is the understanding that I've got nothing and a lot to learn as I jump off into the new assignment God has graciously provided for me. This time, though, I am peaceful and confident. I am certain I will again see His purpose unfold in due time, for I know and believe with every fiber of my being that God is faithful. This time, I enter with no agenda, no self-perpetuated plans lined up. I have issued a directive to myself to stop the madness that is so easy to get caught up in when in this profession. Tucked away are the memories, both good and bad, from this part of my life journey. I will recall them when I am in need of a reminder of God's closeness through all things and at all times. Most of all, I now know that this experience was probably more for my equipping than for any other reason. I will continue the most valuable principle I have learned and that this job required. It supersedes any knowledge or skills I may have used or will ever develop—the principle of the power of loving and caring. I believe in it so strongly because I have seen it empower the lives of the precious people I have worked with.

Long ago someone told me, "People do not care how much you know until they know how much you care." I believe that with all my heart. It is the foundation from which all great organizations and work within them are accomplished.

> *"For I know the plans I have for you," declares the Lord, "plans to prosper*
> *you and not to harm you, plans to give you a hope and a future."*
>
> —*Jeremiah 29:11*

> *Many are the plans in a person's heart, but it is*
> *the Lord's purpose that prevails.*
>
> —*Proverbs 19:21*

CHAPTER 49

Endings and Beginnings

EVERY YEAR, IN THE MONTH of May, I suddenly wake up and say, "Wait a minute! Where did this year go?" It seems the older I become, the faster time passes. Some years are ushered in and go without much change, but that was not the case with this past year. After working as an elementary teacher for seventeen years and an administrator for four, I decided to make another change. A little apprehensive but certain this was the right direction for my life, I returned to the classroom. However, this time I was in very uncharted waters known as middle school. Yes, I did it! Though I loved my years in elementary school in both teaching and administrative roles, this was the missing link for me.

It has been quite a journey, full of unlearning, learning, and relearning. No longer do I open milk cartons in the lunchroom, zip jackets for afternoon play, bandage boo-boos, or explain why it is dangerous to sit backward in your chair with scissors in your mouth. I no longer evacuate buildings for fire drills when a wee one can't resist the temptation to touch that shiny red box on the wall. My days of countless hugs and promises to do the happy dance if they get good behavior reports are things of the past, too.

Yes, being in the middle is definitely different. Now my days are filled with not only academics but also emotions, budding independence, disorganization, and, for the first time, conversations that indicate awareness that they are entitled to their own opinions. Conversations are deeper, values are being shaped, and discipline and diligence are being instilled. Respect for oneself and for others as well and the encouragement to dream big are part of my existence in this new world I have found myself in.

Even when the day leaves me with more questions than answers, I know that there is purpose in this season of life. I trust that God is working out His purpose for me and will complete His work in me in His time. That's why being in the middle is truly amazing!

> *being confident of this, that he who began a good work in you*
> *will carry it on to completion until the day of Christ Jesus.*

—Philippians 1:6

CHAPTER 50

Middles Don't Come with Glue Sticks

A VETERAN TEACHER ONCE TOLD me that being an educator has a recurring perk: "Every year is a chance for a new beginning." At that time, I found this observation to be profound. After all, what other profession offers such a generous opportunity—to be able to start over every August, pick up a clean slate, and ponder the possibilities of the influence you will have in the lives of your students without the baggage of yesteryear? This was just plain ingenious in my book. That is until this past year, when I learned that this principle might need some tweaking from an annual way of thinking.

This past year, I did something most would consider risky. Though it had been well thought out and preceded by much prayer, it was nevertheless radical in the eyes of some. I emptied my desk, packed up my personal possessions, gave up my position as a school administrator, and traded paperwork, policies, and problem solving for the joy of teaching students again. I didn't have to do this; I chose to do this. However, this time it was middle school.

I must admit, when this opportunity was first presented to me, I was a little apprehensive. I thought, *This will be very different.* I likened it to taking up residency in a foreign country. Before much time had passed, I began to realize that I had been wrong. Teaching middles instead of primaries came with a few variations, but overall there really were quite a few commonalities.

On occasion, one-to-one conversations had to happen. My first move in this situation had always been to get eye level. This time around, getting eye level occurred in one of two ways: wearing three-inch heels and sometimes still looking up, or the more familiar method for me of getting on my knees. (The latter

138

required a winch truck to return me to an upright position.) Nevertheless, eye contact is often still very important in the middle school world.

Middles are also always hungry. Snack time in the classroom was a familiar concept for me, so I figured there was no reason it couldn't continue in a middle classroom. After all, primaries aren't the only ones who get hungry. I had three rules: eat nothing that requires more than your fingers, clean up your crumbs, and leave no evidence that you have munched in the classroom. Seemed pretty short and succinct to me. One day as I was making my rounds throughout the classroom, I stopped by a certain middle's desk to find him thoroughly enjoying his "morning snack"—a foot-long sub, to be exact. My first inclination was to define the meaning of the word *snack,* but I caught myself. This *was* his definition of snack. I silently recounted my rules for snacking: *requires nothing more than your fingers to eat, no crumbs (and I didn't see any), and historically, he never left evidence.* I continued my monitoring, and he continued eating what was, in my opinion, his meal. That day I gave in to a new definition for the word *snack.*

Middles, like primaries, give lots of presentations. Some enjoy expounding on their newfound knowledge, while others cringe at the thought of speaking before their peers. This was also true with my primaries. One thing I remembered was the squeakiness of primary voices. I remembered how different their young voices sounded year to year as they moved through the elementary ranks. The same was true for middles. Listening to my first-year middles speak was quite different from hearing my third-years. And somewhere in between, conversations simulated a roller coaster of pitches that caused some vocal bumps in the road during presentations.

Imagination is another area of sameness. Primaries enjoy immensely the sporting of school play or new Halloween costumes. How I missed observing the imaginary duels fighting evil for the good that granted a win just in the nick of time with a strategically placed swipe of the faithful light saber. I also missed the magical moments when self-proclaimed fairy princesses for the day granted a thousand wishes to their followers. I believed these moments were a thing of the past, but I should not have given up quite so quickly, because one day the middles came to class wearing blue surgical gloves they had gotten from the science lab. At first I just observed. It was obvious they were on a mission, making a statement to someone…but who? I didn't know. I watched as they took their seats and prepared to get into the routine. I played along momentarily, but after a brief inquiry into the reason for the addition to the usual school uniform, we agreed that the interesting hand attire would have to be removed for the portion of the class during which it would cause distraction—all of it. I willingly agreed to the wearing of the gloves again at the close of class. After all, lunch followed my class, and the idea of eating in gloves seemed more sanitary than without them.

This year, I discovered middles don't come with glue sticks, or for that matter with scissors, markers, paper, or other art supplies. I suppose it's just not thought to be a middle thing. As it was my first year as a middle, I did the only thing I knew to do. I created community supplies as in the days of old. I reasoned that just because they have crossed over, it shouldn't mean they can't draw, color, cut, or even paste to express their learning. To my surprise, they are quite sophisticated with their drawings, explanations, and overall presentations.

With nearly a year under my belt, I believe it is safe to conclude that being in the middle is just where middles should be at this stage in their lives. It is a time crafted for a special purpose. Though not always an easy place to reside— for me or for them—it is a time of defining and refining both inwardly and outwardly. It is a place where time travel is truly possible. It is acceptable to be able to revisit the comforts of childhood and almost simultaneously move forward with plans for exploring the next level of life—it's a crossroads of sorts. Freely moving between these two worlds for a time is expected. At different times, they make the exchange like a chrysalis—tightly bound, waiting for the perfect time to emerge and say, "I have arrived." This is true also of middles. Middlehood is messy and sometimes confusing; they do not reach maturity in unison. Nevertheless, one by one, in their own time, they withdraw from the ways of childhood. Costumes are traded for conformity and eventually, like the butterfly, beautiful individuality.

I still agree with my friend's statement that educators have the opportunity to begin anew each year, but after a year with middles, I must revise it slightly. For me, beginning again happens much more frequently than once a year. Both middles and myself need the chance to begin again not only yearly but monthly, weekly, daily, and sometimes minute by minute, for it is through this renewal process that they are finding their way to became all that has been purposed for their lives. Middles don't come with glue sticks, but they do come with childhood experiences that should never be negated or tucked away in a box as they become middles. These are the very events that color their ideals, challenge them to imagine what they can be, and glue together a meaningful tapestry from all their experiences in life. Middles are masterpieces in the making.

Yet you, Lord, are our Father.
We are the clay, you are the potter;
we are all the work of your hand.

—Isaiah 64:8

CHAPTER 51

Off the Island

ee⌒⌒2ⁿ⌒

TODAY I WANTED TO VOTE one of my middles right "off the island." It was just a few minutes before the bell rang when I noticed him sauntering into the classroom with a less-than-enthusiastic air about spending the next ninety minutes in class. I watched as he made his way to his desk. Only today he made a deliberate stop at the assignment board. Puzzled, I watched to see why all of a sudden he was so interested in the plans for the day. What happened next, I was not prepared for. This middle ever so slightly lifted his elbow and rather cockily wiped out a bit of the lesson contents and class assignments from the board. Speechless, my mouth wide open, I continued to observe. He shuffled to his seat, set his belongings down, and then picked up his binder and returned to the board. Not realizing I had been watching him from the doorway this entire time, he raised his binder to the board and deliberately erased the majority of the rest of the board's contents. I was shocked!

At this point, I called him out into the hall and addressed the show he had just performed for his classmates, to which he emphatically responded, "I didn't erase anything." By now my sense of tact and reason were quickly flying south. *How dare he stand here and lie about this,* I thought, along with a few other choice things. *Does he really think I am a complete imbecile?* I had seen some irresponsible middle behavior before, but this was so intentional. Standing there, we both claimed disbelief—I couldn't believe he did it, and he claimed he didn't do it! So for that moment, landlocked on any sort of agreement, I somehow managed to remember that I was the adult and it was crucial that I act as such.

I sent him back to the classroom with instructions to re-create with accuracy the contents that had been listed on the board. Next, I summoned a deep breath, self-checked my composure, and reentered the classroom. Rattled, but with self-control now on my side, I informed the class of what to begin working on and told them that I would be placing myself in time-out for a few minutes. I watched from my desk as he labored. The pink, rosy-hued complexion that had aided in giving him such a confident disposition had vanished and been replaced by a pale, colorless skin tone and a lack of confidence unnoticed just moments before. All concentration was on the board as he struggled to re-create the assignments, and I was OK with that. His choices were dictating his consequences. His actions had created a healthy amount of pressure and a reminder to his peers looking on that this thought was one that should have been dismissed rather than executed. Momentarily for me, at least, it was a thing of beauty.

After a few minutes, when I knew my blood pressure had begun its descent back to a normal range and I was pretty sure clarity of mind had returned, class resumed. I was grateful that I'd had the wits about me to put myself in a "holy time-out" rather than expounding on the million and one things I would have liked to have said at that moment. This lapse of time had been just the medicine the doctor ordered—for both of us.

Naturally, I wanted to be his accuser. However, backed into a corner, I knew he would have stubbornly held fast to the false claim that he had no fault in the matter. But now, forced to correct the error of his ways, we had the opportunity to get to the end of this incident. As he attempted to write out the assignments on the board, his handwriting was jerky, uneven, and somewhat disjointed. He wrote, erased, and rewrote the contents several times before getting it just right. We continued the class that day rather unremarkably.

Though I didn't condone what he had done, I truly never wanted him to believe my approval of him would be based on his mistakes rather than his worth to me as a person and as my student, so I called him aside as the class dismissed. It was time to rebuild the rapport between us. That afternoon I replayed the whole scenario over again in my head, remembering that once I had been a middle, too. I hadn't always known why I acted and reacted in certain ways, so why should he? With that reminder, I began to recount the times I had fallen short of the approval of others. It took only a minute or two with that reminder to decide that I need not think about this mishap any longer.

> *Hatred stirs up conflict, but love covers over all wrongs.*

> —PROVERBS 10:12

CHAPTER 52

Middles to the Rescue

IT'S THAT TIME OF YEAR when research projects and the month of May collide, producing a rather cataclysmic feeling in the land of middles. Lengthening days, sunshine, and the awareness that the school year is almost over do nothing to aid the completion of end-of-year research projects. Within the walls of the class-room, strange sounds erupt, including overly exaggerated groaning and deep sighs, and bouts of rolling eyes occur as truth—important truth—is brought to light: the local water park opens before they have seen their last school day for the year.

Middle teachers stick by their beliefs that this peculiar middle behavior is seasonal. It's a passing thing, so they continue their plans as if the school year has just begun. Being a middle newbie, I decided to adopt their frame of mind, not so much because I thought it was the best time of the year to do a research project, but rather because I was in too deep to do otherwise. So the project began. I carefully and consistently modeled the steps of research for this proj-ect. I labored over my explanations. I illustrated with examples and went to great lengths to check understanding, but something was missing. The middles were not connecting the dots in the process. I continued my regimen, but some were focused on finding a direct route to "finished" by way of bypassing every single necessary component. Never mind the fact that I had taught my heart out explaining the process. It was painful for both parties: the middles and me. I knew I had reached an impasse when I came upon their class conversations:

"What?" This all-too-familiar question rolled off their talkative tongues in a convincing tone that was followed quickly by a puzzled look signifying they had never heard such before. This spurred on among them a series of rapid-fire questions that began to shoot forth from their mouths, evoking a certain sense of panic.

* "I have to create note cards first?"
* "Wait, what's a note card?"
* "Can't I just create my presentation and worry about all the steps later?"

I felt myself shrinking back, wishing for that "genie in a bottle" experience to escape the obvious: *they were not listening!* At this point, I was fresh out of explanations; I had no words left. How many times would I have to say it, sing it, write it, demonstrate it, or take some other drastic measure like tap dancing on top of my desk to the research rap just to get an orderly system in place?

Before I could answer my own question, it happened. Just as I began to think I might actually have to sing or even dance to get my points across, a middle who rarely spoke during class raised her hand shyly. I motioned for her to proceed, thinking about the lack of time I really had for input.

"It's like this," she explained. "You have to write the lyrics before you can sing the song."

Though initially it seemed like a random thought, I quickly realized it was a brilliant analogy. The need for order, balance, and just plain old understanding of the importance of a systematic approach in this project, not to mention my utter failure at getting these points across, were all confirmed in a matter of seconds with her insightful words.

It was a miracle. It was "middle language," and they understood.

No longer was there the possibility that I might actually have to resort to drastic measures of tap dancing or torturous repetition for the millionth time. A middle had come to my rescue. We finished the class with understanding and a newfound perspective. God must have a sense of humor. Who knows, maybe while I insist on doing things my way, even when I am less than successful, He shakes His head and extends His hand to help me up onto the desk. I can almost hear Him say, "If you've got to figure it out all by yourself, you might as well dance." Then He motions for me to climb onto the desk. I frown, but I know He is right, and I relent.

I admit I am faulty in this matter. I do everything I can to change a situation, an attitude, or an inevitable outcome. For some reason, I repeatedly make the mistake of believing that I am the only one with answers. I then miss the whispers of wisdom He tries to convey. Why do I choose the lonely, independent road that leads to self-sufficiency and frustration, when what I really need is a rescue? Amazingly, this time it came by way of a middle.

Turn your ear to me, come quickly to my rescue.

—P*salm 31:2*

Jack in the Box

WATCHING JACK RIP INTO PACKAGE after package, seeing his delight in removing every last piece paper from the already bowless packages, was entertaining. He had quite a system going. Rip off all the paper, cast the package aside, and repeat the process. When he was finished, he did have a few favorites that he returned to, but only for a minute or two. What happened next sent the memories of my own early parenting days to the forefront of my mind. Though it had been quite some time ago, it was all too familiar. The new toys had been abandoned; Jack was in a box! Yes, there he was, sitting in a giant box with his package of eight jumbo crayons, just coloring away. The toys had dropped to the bottom, and the cardboard box and crayons had soared to number one on the top-ten-presents list!

More than two thousand years ago, the perfect gift was given to the world. The wrapping paper, a set of swaddling clothes, held the tiniest yet most precious offering—our Savior, Jesus. This gift, though meant for everyone, came with one requirement: choice. Such a magnificent gift can be contained, boxed, and hidden by its recipient; it can be shared, given away, and multiplied; or it can be completely discarded and deemed as rubbish without so much as a thought of its true value. Regardless, a choice is required.

As yet another Christmas season draws to a close, I am thinking, *What will I do with this gift? Will it be my best-kept secret? Will it be shared to bring restoration to a person lost in the shuffle of this world? Will it be deemed useless and without any noteworthy value and lie dormant throughout the year?* I also wonder what you will do with it. Together, we can choose to *remember the gift, share the gift,* and *live in the power of this remarkable gift.*

Thanks be to God for his indescribable gift!

—*2 Corinthians 9:15*

SUGGESTED READING

Young, Sarah. *Jesus Calling: Enjoying Peace in His Presence: Devotions for Every Day of the Year*. Nashville, TN: Integrity Publishers, 2004.

Note: The website Biblegateway.com is extremely helpful for those who wish to study the Bible or quote the Bible in published works. It provides many different translations of the Holy Bible, searchable by chapter and verse and also by keywords.

Made in the USA
Lexington, KY
11 March 2017